Also by Elisabeth Beresford

Invisible Magic

Elisabeth Beresford

Dangerous Magic

Illustrated by Oliver Chadwick

DRAGON
GRANADA PUBLISHING
London Toronto Sydney New York

Published by Granada Publishing Limited
in Dragon Books 1978

ISBN 0 583 30268 8

First published in 1972 by Rupert Hart-Davis Ltd

Granada Publishing Limited
Frogmore, St Albans, Herts AL2 2NF
and
3 Upper James Street, London W1R 4BP
1221 Avenue of the Americas, New York, NY 10020, USA
117 York Street, Sydney, NSW 2000, Australia
100 Skyway Avenue, Toronto, Ontario, Canada M9W 3A6
Trio City, Coventry Street, Johannesburg 2001, South Africa
CML Centre, Queen and Wyndham, Auckland 1, New Zealand

Made and printed in Great Britain by
Richard Clay (The Chaucer Press) Ltd
Bungay Suffolk
Set in Linotype Baskerville

FOR
ELYSE FIONA KIRSTY CHADWICK

Contents

1. *The Storm*

The thunderstorm rumbled and grumbled to itself up and down the Thames for most of the day. However, as Londoners don't usually take much notice of the weather, and why should they when they can always escape from it down the nearest Underground station, nobody worried about it too much. People wore their mackintoshes to work, policemen kept their waterproof capes handy and children were sent off to school muffled up to the eyebrows as though their mothers expected a snowstorm rather than a possible downpour of rain, but apart from these few precautions nobody was particularly interested in what was going on several hundred feet above their heads.

Of course there were a few exceptions. Some people cannot help being very nervous about thunderstorms. They are quite sure in their own minds that the lightning is certain to come zig-zagging down to earth in order to hit exactly the place which they happen to be standing on at the time, and so these people either hurried to work, or did the shopping as fast as they could, or else flatly refused to go out of doors at all and drew their curtains and turned up their radios as loudly as possible—and even in some cases covered their mirrors with blankets or tablecloths or whatever happened to come in handy.

'What's the point of doing it, anyway?' Sammy Jenkins asked his Uncle Ted as the two of them, carrying three thick grey blankets apiece, entered the lift of Block Three, Leo Mansions.

'Search me,' replied Uncle Ted, 'something to do with the lightning making for its own reflection I daresay. Lot of nonsense anyway. You can work the lift if you want.'

'Thanks. Now?'

Uncle Ted took a look at the deserted entrance hall and nodded as he shut the lift doors with a click. Usually Sammy wasn't allowed to ride in the lift, let alone work it, as it was meant for the people who lived in the flats only. The people who paid rent that is, as Uncle Ted was the caretaker of this block and himself had a large, rather gloomy flat in the basement which Sammy also shared, together with Uncle Ted's wife, Sammy's Aunt Jessie, fourteen budgerigars, ten goldfish and eight very small turtles. All these animals were kept as a deep, dark secret as pets were not allowed at Leo Mansions. In fact two of the blankets which Sammy was now carrying were normally kept to throw over the cages of the budgerigars when nosey visitors arrived. Once shrouded in the blankets the budgerigars always stopped singing and quarrelling between themselves as they apparently believed that night-time had suddenly descended on them and it was therefore correct to go to sleep in silence. Luckily there were very few unexpected visitors, otherwise the budgerigars might have become very mixed up in their own small minds and to Sammy it was always rather thrilling when Uncle Ted rapped out the order.

'Blankets!'

It was, in a way, as though they were harbouring an escaped prisoner in the basement flat and it gave him shivers up and down his spine. He had the shivers a bit at this particular moment too as there was a funny feeling in the air. The lift creaked upwards to the sixth floor, pausing for breath as it always did between the fourth and fifth, and then with a triumphant 'psssssssh' it reached the top of Leo Mansions. Although it was only the middle of the afternoon the sky was quite dark and Uncle Ted and Sammy went to look out of the landing window. Below them was the even darker square of grass and trees which was Unicorn Gardens. It had high railings all the way round it and four gates, all of them locked. The only people who had keys to these were those who lived in Leo Mansions and none of them were making use of this privilege at the moment so the gardens were completely deserted.

'It's going to be a storm and a half,' Uncle Ted said, 'my word it is. Hope your Aunt Jessie'll get home before it breaks.'

'Um. I like it. I mean like the feeling of it,' said Sammy, breathing heavily on the glass. 'It's sort of—of exciting.'

'Ah, that'll be the electricity in the air. *They* won't care for it too much though.'

'They' meant the animals down in the basement and indeed the birds had been strangely silent most of the day, hunching up their feathers and making small tut-tutting sounds instead of singing. Even the goldfish and the turtles had been unusually slow in their movements.

'I wonder if it minds,' Sammy said, more to himself than to his Uncle, and he screwed up his eyes against the grey-yellow gloom and tried to make out the figure of the small statue which stood in the centre of the garden and gave it its name. But the marble Unicorn had almost faded from sight, and there was just the faintest glimmer of white, more of a whitish blob really, that showed where it stood, with two of its hooves pawing impatiently at the London air and its head, with one long horn right in the middle of its forehead, thrown back. It always seemed to Sammy that the Unicorn was impatient to get away, as though if only one knew how, it could be set free to gallop off. He had never told anybody this, not even Uncle Ted or Aunt Jessie, because he wasn't sure that even they would understand.

'Well, we'd best get on,' said Uncle Ted, 'by the sound of things it's getting late.'

They could always tell the time of day by the beat

of the traffic from north to south down the Earls Court Road which was only one street away from the flats. It was one of the busiest thoroughfares in London and even at three or four in the morning there was always a roar of engines, but in morning and evening rush hours the roar slowed down to a steady thud-thud, rather like the sound of surf breaking on a shore.

Uncle Ted knocked on the door of Flat Number 21 and it was opened at once by a small girl with a very white face, only in the murky light of the storm she looked grey-yellow.

'We've brought the blankets for your mirrors,' Uncle Ted said, 'I'm the caretaker, Mr Jenkins.'

The girl didn't say anything but as she stood aside a very agitated voice called out.

'Jenkins, Jenkins is that you? Come in, come in. Oh dear, oh dear it's a very nasty storm isn't it? I do wish we weren't on the *very* top floor. In here, in here . . .'

An old woman, who was as small as the girl, appeared in the hall of the flat. She was dressed in black and had a long stick which she leant on with both hands.

'If you would be so kind as to cover up the looking-glass in the front room, Jenkins, it would make me feel so much easier in my mind. In here, in here . . . hallo, who are you? Oh yes, you're Sammy aren't you? And you've got blankets too. How kind. How very kind. In here, in here . . .'

It was quite a business fixing the blankets over all the mirrors, but Uncle Ted was very good with his hands and he'd had the foresight to bring with him a hammer and some tacks so that within quite a short time every piece of glass was covered, and as he worked Uncle Ted kept talking in his slow soothing voice so that at the finish the old woman said.

'I daresay you think I'm very foolish, but when I was a girl I was caught in a particularly bad storm out in India. I was riding at the time and my pony was killed and it gave me such a *fear* of lightning. I was particularly fond of that pony too.'

'Yes, yes,' Uncle Ted said, 'I quite see how it is. Well, you'll be all right and tight now Mrs Barnes with nothing to fret about. Anyway, when the tide turns maybe the storm'll go with it down river to Greenwich, maybe even as far as the estuary. Come along then Sammy.'

'Why aren't you at school?' the girl asked, speaking for the first time.

'I'm in quarantine. Mumps.'

The girl's eyes grew rounder than before and then to Sammy's surprise she stopped looking so serious and giggled.

'So am I,' she said, 'and it's very boring because there's nothing to do and no one to talk to except Granny. I wish . . .' She paused and Sammy, who hadn't much liked the look of her at first but who now felt that they had mumps in common, was tempted to ask if she'd like to come down to the basement. Then he remembered the budgerigars, the goldfish and the turtles so he only replied.

'Well, it's only three weeks. You're not frightened about the storm are you?'

''Course not,' the girl replied, but all the same Sammy had the feeling that she didn't really feel quite as brave as she pretended to be. He would have liked to say something cheerful to buck her up, but he couldn't think of anything in particular so he only smiled and followed Uncle Ted out onto the landing and pressed the bell for the lift. It took a long time to cough its way to the fifth floor and the reason for this became obvious when the lift finally appeared and the doors were pushed back and a small but stout gentleman got out.

'This lift,' he said, waving a podgy finger under Uncle Ted's nose, 'is most inefficient. Most. I shall complain to the landlords. It became very slow between the fourth and fifth floors. Please see to it.'

'It always does, Mr Dimitriadi . . .' began Uncle Ted, but the stout gentleman had waddled away and was fitting his key into the front door of Number 22, so Uncle Ted only winked slightly at Sammy and pulled open the lift gates.

'Always a one to complain *he* is,' said Uncle Ted as they sank slowly towards the basement. 'Never anything right for him, there isn't. Hallo, here comes the thunder again if I'm not much mistaken. Let's hope your Aunt gets back ahead of the rain, eh?'

As it happened she did, as did most of London's day workers, for although the storm continued to rumble away overhead not a drop of rain fell during the evening, although the birds—with no blankets to cover them either—continued to be unusually quiet and the television set kept getting streaky lines across it. Sammy still had the same shivery feeling up and down his back when he went to bed, but he fell asleep fast enough and was dreaming about being at the sea-side when suddenly . . .

CRASH, BANG, CRACK.

The tide might have turned, but the storm had obviously not decided to follow the slow movement of the Thames towards the open sea. Having hovered in such a threatening manner all day over London it now let go with all the force and power at its command. The thunder rattled every window over ten square miles, rattled it until each pane of glass shook and shivered and then the lightning went off like a gigantic fireworks exhibition. It hissed through the skies in flashing fingers of brilliance and even quite brave people pulled the blankets over their heads, and some got up and made themselves cups of tea.

Sammy, who like thousands of his fellow Londoners was somewhere between the two, got out of bed and pulled aside the curtain of his bedroom to watch the fun. It really was something to see, both fascinating and scaring at the same time because for a second everything would be black as the deepest black and the next it would all be lit up with a whiteness that hurt the eyes.

'My word,' said Sammy, 'I say. Gosh. *That* was a big one.'

And then, quite clearly from his semi-basement bedroom at the back of Leo Mansions he saw one zig-zag of lightning come streaking down out of the sky till with a truly terrible hissing sound it touched the very centre of the Gardens, seemed to hover for a moment and then vanished.

It was so vivid that Sammy shut his eyes but even so he could see the brilliance against his eyelids and for just one second he saw, or thought he saw, a white head jerk backwards and four hooves completely leave the ground, and then his Aunt Jessie had switched on the ordinary flat light and was saying; 'Are you all right, ducky? *Wasn't* that a bang. I've put on the milk so we can all have a nice hot drink . . .'

'But . . .' said Sammy, who was staring out into the deep black darkness that had now clamped down on the Gardens. 'But . . .' and then he shrugged himself into the nice warm dressing-gown that Aunt Jessie was holding out for him and tied up the cord and followed her out of his bedroom and along to the kitchen.

Because how could he tell her—and anyway he wasn't exactly sure that he'd seen it—that the last flash of zig-zag lightning had come straight down on the statue of the unicorn and that the unicorn itself had soared clean away from its stand and out into the black night of Earls Court?

'I imagined it,' Sammy said to himself, 'it didn't really happen. 'Course not . . .'

The rain had started to fall, thundering down, plonk, plonk, plonk, sending up little rainbow splashes as it hit the roofs, roads and pavements.

'What a storm, eh?' said Uncle Ted, 'The milk's coming up to the boil, Jess.'

'What a storm,' agreed Sammy, taking a nice comforting mug of chocolate between his hands. He leant back and lifted a corner of the kitchen curtain and looked out at the arrows of water which were beating against the panes.

He couldn't see much, because his eyes were still dazzled by the lightning so that the amber glow of the street lamps appeared to be very dull.

All the same he could make out one thing for certain through the basement railings. The marble square stone in the centre of Unicorn Gardens appeared to be empty, and there seemed to be no sign of the Unicorn.

'Well . . .' said Sammy to the budgerigars who were just starting to wake up and chirp to each other. 'Well . . .'

But it wasn't well at all, for this was only the beginning. . . .

2. *The Vanishing Unicorn*

Sammy overslept the following morning in spite of the fact that the budgerigars were singing twice as loudly as usual to make up for their silence of the day before. Aunt Jessie decided that the best thing was to 'let him lay' as she put it and so she went off to work while Uncle Ted took the lift up to the top floor to retrieve his blankets and Sammy, unaware of all this, slept happily on.

Mrs Bates had managed to unhook most of the blankets with the aid of her stick and her granddaughter Eleanor was stacking them in a rather untidy heap just inside the front door when Uncle Ted arrived. She looked a bit pale so he said kindly.

'Hallo, did the storm keep you awake then?'

'A bit. It was ever so loud wasn't it?'

'Not half.'

Eleanor tossed back her long hair and screwed up her mouth because she was thinking deeply. She'd never met Mr Jenkins before yesterday evening, but all the same there are some people you feel you can trust and some who you know would laugh at you or not even listen. However, she had a feeling that Mr Jenkins was somebody you could tell practically anything to and it would be all right. But while she was working all this out in her mind her grandmother came hurrying down the passage and the moment was lost.

'Ah, Mr Jenkins, there you are, there you are. What a storm!'

'Terrible wasn't it?'

'I thought the roof was coming in. I was so glad of your blankets. There's just one I can't get down and it's too high even for Nell to reach so if you could give me a hand . . .'

'Yes, of course.'

'Good, good, it's in the front room. Nell could take the other blankets down to the basement for you. She knows how to work the lift . . .'

'Well I'm not sure . . .' began Uncle Ted who had suddenly remembered how lively the budgerigars were feeling this morning, but Eleanor had already scooped up the pile of blankets and vanished out of the flat. She didn't bother about taking the lift but ran down and round the stairs with her sandals slapping. It was a wonderful feeling to be free and out of the top flat and she went faster and faster until she was quite giddy by the time she reached the basement.

The sound of the bell, which was extremely loud, roused Sammy from his sleep and he pulled on his dressing-gown and got out of bed without bothering to open his eyes. They were still half shut when he opened the front door.

'S'me,' said Eleanor somewhat indistinctly from behind the blankets.

'Who's me?' asked Sammy, rubbing some of the sleep out of his eyes.

'Me,' replied Eleanor and dropped the blankets with a thud, 'I say, what's the noise?'

'It's the birds of course . . . oh.'

Sammy reached for a blanket to throw over that tell-tale cage and then realised it was too late for that. His brain wasn't thinking very fast at the moment so he said the only thing which came into his head.

'Come in.'

Eleanor stepped over the blankets and followed Sammy down the dark passage to the large back room that housed the budgerigars, the fish and the turtles. As she had obviously heard the birds it was no good trying to hide anything else and Sammy was still too muddle-headed to work out any other ideas.

'I say,' said Eleanor, 'are they all yours?'

'No.'

'I've got some hens at home; well, they aren't mine *exactly*, because we keep them for their eggs, but they're not very clever and you can't teach them tricks. Do these birds do tricks?'

'No.'

The conversation seemed to have come to a full stop .so Eleanor and Sammy stared at the birds in silence until the budgerigars got quite shy and started preening their feathers and going 'tut tut tut' as they fluttered round their enormous cage.

'Look here.'

'I say.'

Both Nell and Sammy said together and then there was a further few seconds when they kept saying 'No you,' 'no honestly you say', because like the birds they were uneasy and shy.

'Oh all right, look here,' said Eleanor frowning fiercely through the bars at a particularly handsome blue budgerigar which turned its small back and tried to pretend it was invisible, 'look here, I know you'll laugh and you'll think I'm cracked. Off my head. Nutty. But . . .'

'Go on,' Sammy said encouragingly as Eleanor dried up, 'like a cup of coffee?'

'Um. Last night I wasn't asleep because of the storm. The thunder was right over us you know. It made everything in the flat shake. One of granny's vases nearly fell off the shelf. It was awful, so you do see that I couldn't possibly have dreamed it.'

Sammy very sensibly decided that the girl from the top flat was going to spend ages and ages going round the point before she got to it so he nodded and filled up the kettle, lit the gas and got the mugs and the catering size jar of instant coffee and had doled out a spoonful apiece and was opening the fridge door for the milk when Eleanor said with a great spurt.

'It landed on my balcony.'

'What did? The lightning?'

'No. Don't be silly. It. From there.'

Eleanor suddenly deserted the cage and ran across to the basement window and pointed to the bushes round the gardens which were still glistening with rain. Only a small portion of the bushes was visible as the United Dairies milk float had drawn up on the pavement and was effectively blocking the view.

'What IT?' asked Sammy, adding, 'One sugar or two?'

'One. It. That animal in the middle of the lawn. Like a horse only it's got a long horn thing between its ears. Rather like a lady's umbrella.'

'That's a unicorn,' Sammy said in a stern voice. 'Don't you know a unicorn when you see one? It's not a horse at all and as for umbrellas . . . you *what*?'

'I saw it on my balcony. It landed there quite suddenly with a sort of thud. My window wasn't quite shut because Granny said the glass might break if it was too tightly closed and the wind had blown the curtains a bit apart. There'd just been a very very bright flash of lightning and some thunder so I shut my eyes and then there was this other noise and some gasping . . .'

'Gasping . . .' Sammy said faintly. He was starting to gasp a bit himself.

'Yes, gasping. Like you do when you've been running. The kettle's boiling; so of course I looked. I thought it was a big bird, a swan or something and it *was* sort of like that because it's white. Only it was the uni—? Uni?'

'Corn.'

'That's right.'

'Get on,' Sammy said after a long pause during which he had made the coffee and presented one mug to Eleanor together with a plastic spoon.

'There you are, you see,' Eleanor replied with a

kind of melancholy triumph, 'you don't believe me. You think I'm nutty. I knew you would, only I had to tell somebody and I thought you might understand more than other people. Might,' she added, not quite certain that she had made her meaning plain.

Sammy perched on the edge of the kitchen table, handed his guest a digestive biscuit, bit into one himself and surveyed his own bare feet swinging backwards and forwards above the vinyl floor. He knew perfectly well that he was awake, because it was his experience that you can't eat and drink in dreams, especially very hot coffee which burns the roof of your mouth. So all this was really happening and that meant either the girl from the top flat was bonkers or that she was telling the truth.

'What happened then?' he asked cautiously, one eye on the door. People who got funny ideas could be dangerous, so he'd heard, and although the girl was smaller and skinnier than he was, he wasn't sure that he'd be able to manage if she started shouting or throwing things about.

'Not much. It—the unicorn animal—gasped for a bit more and then it turned itself round. It was a very tight fit for it on the balcony so its face was right up against my window and it looked—it looked—sad. Then it went away.'

'You mean it fell off?'

'No it didn't do that. It sort of pushed with its feet and went up and sideways. I couldn't see very clearly because the sky was black and there wasn't any lightning. I suppose the storm was getting over by then. There'd been an awful bang just before, the worst bang of them all. Oh well.'

Eleanor put her empty mug down beside the sink and moved slowly towards the door. She had her hand on the knob when Sammy said suddenly.

'Stop. Hold on a tick. I remember—only I thought afterwards that I'd made it up—that I saw the unicorn had gone from its stand. Of course it can't have done unless the lightning made it break into bits. Oh bother that milk van. Look here, hold on *two* ticks and I'll get dressed. Have another biscuit or something.'

'Yes, but—but do you believe me then?'

'Can't say, not sure. Just wait.'

As Sammy was an expert in getting dressed in under a minute Eleanor had only just finished washing up both mugs when he returned and said curtly.

'Come on.'

'Where to?'

'Your flat. Better use the stairs, because I'm not supposed to go in the lift except with Uncle Ted.'

'Yes, but why . . .'

'Oh don't keep asking things. I say, what's your name?'

'Eleanor, but most people call me Nell. Sometimes they call me Little Nell—that's out of Dickens you know—because I'm short, but I don't like it. I'll probably grow like anything one day. You *do* believe me, don't you?'

'Sort of.'

Sammy led the way up the stairs and beckoned to Nell to keep quiet as the lift wheezed past them on its downward journey. They stood back against the wall and heard two familiar voices speaking.

'Yes, it was a very bad storm, sir. Worst as I can remember.'

'Uncle Ted,' breathed Sammy and then the other person in the lift replied.

'I do not believe that the lightning conductors in these flats are completely efficient. I shall complain to the landlords, caretaker. I mean to take . . .'

'Mr Dimitriadi,' said Nell, giggling, 'he's always on about something.'

The front door of Number 21 was not fastened so they were able to slide into the flat without making a noise. A vacuum cleaner was being used very energetically in the furthest room and Nell said soundlessly:

'Granny. This way.'

Nell's bedroom was at the back and looked directly over the gardens. It was a small room with one window which had a tiny balcony jutting out from it. A balcony just about big enough to hold two people if they stood side by side.

Sammy pushed up the window frame and looked out. The stonework gleamed in the pale sunlight and there were muddy marks on it. Sammy, feeling like a detective, leaned out and looked at them. There was no doubt about it, there were strange hoof-type marks in the grime. The kind of marks which could have been made by a creature trying to get some sort of foothold in a small space.

'There,' Nell said triumphantly, 'see!'

'Yes, but,' agreed Sammy and then narrowing his eyes against the light, 'but look down there,' and he pointed to the gardens dozens of feet below them. They had a bird's-eye view up here and could see not only the railings, the bushes and the four paths which led to the centre of the gardens, but also the statue in the middle.

It was the Unicorn all right, its two front feet poised well into the air, its head thrown back and its one horn etched against the dark green grass.

'There,' Sammy repeated, 'it hasn't moved. You must have dreamt it. We both must. Only . . .'

'Oh dear . . . only what?'

'It's tail isn't the same. I *know* the Unicorn, I've looked at it often and often and it's not in the same place. Oh look . . .'

Sammy and Nell both leant perilously far over the stone sill as one of the garden gates was pushed open and a small, round figure carrying several objects strode purposefully into the garden.

'It's Mr Dimitriadi,' whispered Nell and suddenly she shivered. 'He's going to see the Unicorn and I don't like it.'

'Neither do I much,' agreed Sammy, 'come on, let's go and find out what it's all about.'

3. The Unicorn . . .

Mr Dimitriadi opened out a small green camping stool and sat down on it with great care. The legs of the stool creaked a bit and its feet sank several inches into the wet turf, but the seat itself held firm and Mr Dimitriadi reached down, unzipped the airline bag at his side and pulled out a large pad of white paper and some felt-tipped pens. It was quite chilly in the Gardens in spite of the sunshine, but Mr Dimitriadi did not appear to notice this. In fact for once he was in a very good temper and he sang softly to himself as he looked up at the white statue of the Unicorn.

'Elysian Fields my long lost home,
Where shall I ever find you?
Must I wander the whole wide . . .'

A shadow fell across his drawing and Mr Dimitriadi stopped singing and looked round quickly. A boy and girl were standing behind him, but as they were between him and the sun he couldn't see their faces properly.

'Go away, go away,' Mr Dimitriadi said irritably, waving one of the pens. 'This place is private property and you are not allowed here. Unless you leave at once I shall call the caretaker and get him to throw you out. Go, go!'

'Please,' said Sammy, 'we *are* allowed here. It's me you know, and my Uncle Ted's the caretaker. And this is Nell from the top floor.'

Mr Dimitriadi put up his hand to shield his eyes and then smiled. It wasn't much of a smile, but it was a lot better than his previous angry expression.

'Oh yes,' he said, 'all the same, will you please move to one side. You're in my light and I have some very important work to do.'

Sammy and Nell exchanged rather surprised glances at this as the 'work' appeared to be some rather splodgy drawings of the Unicorn. In fact Nell, who was rather good at drawing herself, felt she could have done rather better. However it seemed a bit on the rude side to say so and she and Sammy walked on, glancing over their shoulders at the statue as they did so.

'It looks the same to me,' Nell said in a low voice. 'I know I didn't dream it, but I suppose I must have. After all statues can't fly, can they?'

'Never heard of any doing it,' Sammy agreed, 'but it's very peculiar all the same, both of us dreaming the same dream. And the unicorn does look different somehow. Let's hang about for a bit and then when Mr D. goes we can get closer. O.K?'

But Mr Dimitriadi, it transpired, was much better at hanging about than they were. He might not be much good as an artist, but he was certainly very determined to try and improve and by lunch time he was still there in spite of a chill wind blowing across the gardens. The gardens themselves were really rather dull and there was nothing to do except walk round and round them and to play games like 'I Spy' and to ask each other questions. Sammy told Nell about his father who was an engineer working out in Kuwait where it was so hot that if you went out in the sun at midday you were cooked through and through.

'Your blood turns into gravy,' Sammy said, a statement which made Nell's eyes go round as buttons. Rather pleased with this reaction, Sammy went on, 'One day I'm going to be an engineer too and then I'll travel all over the world just like my Dad. He's with a firm called U.O.D.T. and they send people just anywhere. But . . .' and he heaved a big sigh and kicked at a stone on the neat gravel path.

'But . . .' asked Nell, who was longing to talk about herself, but was polite enough to let Sammy have his say first.

'Well, I don't half wish my Dad'd come home for a holiday. He's been gone for ages and ages. When you go to Kuwait you have to say you'll stay there for a long time you see. It's got something to do with bonuses.'

'What's that?'

'Money, I think. Mind,' Sammy added hastily, 'it's ever so nice being with Uncle Ted and Aunt Jessie, but it's not the same.'

'I know.'

They turned a corner of the path and had to step aside for a girl who was pushing a pram. She was a grown-up girl, but only a bit taller than Sammy, and wearing a bright red scarf over her head and tucked round her waist. She bowed and smiled and passed on and Nell said in a whisper.

'She's nice. She works at Number 23. She's an "O Pear".'

'A what?'

'O Pear. That's what Granny calls her. She looks after the baby of the people who live in the flat. Haven't you got a mother?'

'No.'

'Oh. Well I have. We live on a farm in Hampshire quite near the New Forest. I've got a baby brother too. But what I'd really like is a pony. I love riding more than practically anything else in the world. One day my father says I may have a pony of my very own and then I can ride and ride all the time, except when I'm at school. But a pony costs a lot of money. It's very dull here, isn't it?'

'Yes,' Sammy agreed with a great deal of feeling, 'It's just about the dullest place in the whole world. Is Mr D. still drawing?'

'Yes.'

'I tell you what, let's go and look up Unicorns in the encyclopedia.'

The encyclopedia in question was twenty volumes dated 1929 which Uncle Ted kept in a special bookcase. Their particular volume TEXT—VASC was not much help as it merely referred to the Unicorn as a mythical creature with magical powers, but was rather vague as to what these powers might be.

'Granting strength,' read Sammy, 'and its horn was highly valued by the Ancients. Oh well. Let's play something else. Is he *still* there?'

He was, perched on his camping stool and drawing away for all he was worth while the only other person in the Gardens was the little 'O Pear' girl and her pram. Nell went upstairs for her lunch and then rejoined Sammy for the afternoon. Both of them felt rather let down as though something which had started as an exciting adventure had turned into a false alarm and the only highspot in an afternoon spent playing Monopoly (which Sammy won quite easily) was when Nell said suddenly, 'The lion and the unicorn, fighting for the crown. I read that somewhere. Isn't it odd that this should be Leo Mansions? Leo is another word for lion you know.'

'Yes, I did. I've landed on the Old Kent Road, how much do I owe you?'

It was nearly dark when the game was finished and both of them had almost forgotten the Unicorn when they heard the gates of the Gardens clang shut and then footsteps followed by the whine of the lift going upwards. They looked at each other and then Sammy said.

'Come on, one more try,' and took the Gardens' key off the hook.

It was decidedly cold by now and Nell shivered as they let themselves into the darkness of the Gardens. They were not very well lit and to her it seemed as though the shadowy bushes were full of all kinds of strange shapes. Even the rush hour traffic up and down the Earls Court Road was only a distant roar and she walked so close to Sammy she kept treading on his heels. The Unicorn was poised against the night sky, its front hooves well off the ground and its tail flying out behind it. There was something rather proud and beautiful about it and without really thinking Nell said softly:

'Elysian Fields, my long lost home
Where shall I ever find you . . .'

And then she stopped and gripped hold of Sammy's arm because without a shadow of doubt the marble statue had moved. It wasn't just a trick of the flying clouds behind it either as one hoof with quite a large 'click' came to rest on its marble plinth. And then very slowly, but most gracefully, the other front leg descended as well and the head of the Unicorn turned and looked towards them. There was a very, very long silence between the three of them and then Sammy heard his own voice saying in a somewhat wobbly manner.

'H—hallo.'

The Unicorn bent its beautiful white head even lower, until it was quite close to Sammy's (and Sammy's face was just as pale at this moment), and then it said somewhat indistinctly.

'Who calls?'

It was a strange sort of voice. It had an echo in it and yet at the same time it was rather muffled.

'I did,' said Sammy, 'at least, she did. Nell that is. I say you are a statue aren't you?'

'Not any more,' the Unicorn replied and flicked its ears and then its tail. 'Are you friend or enemy?'

'I'm not sure,' Sammy replied. At this particular moment in time he was not sure of anything at all so he reached out and took hold of Nell's hand which was shaky, but reassuringly warm.

'White magic or black?' asked the Unicorn in its oddly sweet but husky voice. 'You must know *that*.'

'Wh-wh-wh-wh,' said Sammy, 'I mean white. I think. Black's bad isn't it?'

'So they say,' the Unicorn let out such a terrific sigh that even its tail quivered against the racing dark grey sky. 'But personally I'm never too certain of anything. Do you mind if I move about a little? I'm so stiff. That small man has been watching me all day so I dared not move again. I do not like *him*—he made me uneasy . . .'

It stretched out first one long graceful leg and then another while Sammy and Nell watched it, both their mouths so wide open that they made black shadows in their pale faces.

'There, that's better. I cannot tell you what a relief it is to move. When one has been standing still for such a very long time, one does get a bit stuck. Now then, tell me about the Elysian Fields.'

'The—the what?' Nell asked timidly. It was one thing to long for some kind of adventure and quite another when it actually happens, especially when you know you are right in the middle of London with the rush hour traffic only a short distance away. Magic, after all, should only take place in very special places.

'The Elysian Fields,' the Unicorn repeated, 'you were singing about them only a very short while ago you know. I heard you.' And it put its beautiful white head close to Nell's. It had calm, rather blank eyes and Nell found herself replying.

'I'm afraid I only heard somebody else singing that. I don't know what it means really.'

To Nell's dismay two large shining tears squeezed out of the corners of the Unicorn's eyes and it snorted softly.

'Don't, oh please don't,' Nell said, reaching out one hand to touch the cold and shining mane. 'I hate people crying.'

'I'm not crying and I'm not people. I'm a Unicorn. The last, the very last Unicorn and I want to go home where I belong. Won't you help me?'

'We would if we could, but we don't know how,' Sammy said helplessly. 'Where is your home anyway?'

'The Elysian Fields, of course.' One delicate hoof stamped impatiently on the marble plinth and the white mane was tossed against the hurrying night sky. There was an unusual clicking sound and then the briefest silence which was followed by a rapid 'tick-tick-tick-tick-tick' which suddenly reminded Sammy of the day when the windshield of his Uncle Ted's car had been shattered by a stone. It was as though a sheet of ice had begun to melt very fast and, in fact, that was exactly what it looked like too, for the marble plinth was quite literally cracking up into smaller and still smaller pieces. The flash of lightning which had zig-zagged down out of the storm to bring the Unicorn back to life hadn't done its stand any good at all and that delicate stamping of one hoof had completed the job. The Unicorn stared down at its disolving platform and Sammy, with great presence of mind, caught hold of its cold white mane and dragged it clear otherwise it might have had a nasty fall.

'Oh dear,' the creature said, trembling and snorting, 'oh dear, how very unpleasant. *Now* what shall I do?'

It turned to look at Sammy who was glancing anxiously round the dark Gardens just in case the cracking up of the marble had been witnessed by some old lady out walking her dog. But there was no one else about and Sammy, recovering from the second shock he'd had within a few minutes, turned back to find that both the Unicorn and Nell were watching him hopefully.

'*Do*?' Sammy said, 'well, can't you stay here?'

'Oh no. If I haven't got a beautiful plinth to stand on everybody will know I'm not a statue. You will have to find me somewhere else to hide. You must protect me, after all, it's your *duty*. There's always been somebody to look after me, because I'm so precious.'

Sammy was so stunned by these words that he could not think of any answer at all. Keeping the budgerigars, the fish and the turtles a secret was difficult enough and the prospect of finding somewhere to hide a full-grown, shining white unicorn seemed quite impossible.

'There are those little shed places by your back door,' said Nell, patting and stroking the Unicorn in an attempt to stop it trembling so much. It rested its head on her shoulder and snorted gently in her ear. Its breath was as cold as the wind off a snow-topped mountain.

'Those are coal sheds,' Sammy replied. 'That is they used to be when the people in the flats had real fires and not central heating.'

'Well, what's kept in them now?'

'Nothing much. Oh all right, we'll try. But if we get caught Uncle Ted'll probably lose his job or something awful.'

'We won't *get* caught,' Nell said firmly, 'Come on Unicorn dear.'

'But quietly,' Sammy whispered, 'please be as quiet as you possibly can.'

'All right, lead me to my new apartments,' the

Unicorn said. It had recovered from both its sudden burst of temper and its fright with remarkable speed and was now gazing rather aimlessly round the dark Gardens. It went on, 'And then once I'm safe you can get on with your next task.'

'What?'

Sammy paused just short of the garden gate and turned to look into the creature's beautiful, placid eyes.

'Why, finding the Elysian Fields for me. Otherwise I should have to stay with you for ever and ever and I wouldn't really care for that.'

It occurred to Sammy at the same moment that he wouldn't care for it much himself. Already he was aware of a growing certainty in his own mind that the Unicorn was going to be something of a problem.

4. . . . and the Lion

'Isn't it odd,' Nell said, 'how we weren't surprised when the Unicorn first talked to us? It seemed quite ordinary somehow. It's a very *beautiful* creature, isn't it?'

'Yes, and stupid,' replied Sammy absentmindedly. They had managed to install the Unicorn in the largest of the ex-coal sheds. It was a very clean shed, but the Unicorn obviously hadn't thought much of the furnishings which were made up of several ancient and very large trunks, a stuffed stag's head, a baby's high chair and some rather battered cardboard boxes.

'Not quite what I've been used to, but very welcome of course,' it said, tossing its handsome head.

'Better than being out in the rain and the snow and the cold in the Gardens though,' replied Sammy somewhat crossly.

'Ah, but the climate doesn't bother me, I just don't feel it. And there, in the Gardens, I was in the very centre you know.'

'Meaning,' said Sammy in an undertone to Nell, 'that people could stand and admire it. Well, the fewer people who see it at the moment the better so it'll just have to admire itself.'

And Sammy had stumped off and got out the somewhat speckled mirror that was usually kept in the junk cupboard under the stairs. It had BUY BOOFERS BACON IT'S BEST painted round the edges, but the Unicorn noticed neither this nor the speckles for the moment it saw its own beautiful reflection it stopped fidgeting and stood quite still staring into its own white eyes until at last it let out a deep, happy sigh and snorted gently.

'I suppose your Uncle hasn't got a curry comb?' Nell asked.

'A what?'

Sammy was giving the budgerigars their evening feed with a deep frown between his eyes. Nell appeared to have taken the magical reawakening of the Unicorn from marble into life—even if it was ice-cold life—as quite an everyday occurrence. Perhaps the fact that she was a couple of years younger than Sammy had something to do with it, she just didn't question things, but merely accepted them. Sammy, however, was a practically-minded boy, not particularly clever, but slow and thorough and he was still absorbing the surprise of it all. Added to which he foresaw quite clearly that it was going to be impossible to keep the Unicorn hidden for long. The best possible thing to do was to find these blessed Elysian Fields that it kept chattering on about. So Sammy got down the A to Z of London streets and turned to the index.

'A curry comb,' repeated Nell, 'it's for brushing down horses and ponies with. I should like to get the Unicorn's coat really glossy.'

'Bother, not there,' Sammy said shutting the book with a slap, 'well, it was only a small chance. What on earth do we do *next*?'

In fact they had no chance at all to work out any further plans of action as Aunt Jessie came bustling back from the supermarket where she worked, and had to be introduced to Nell who suddenly realised she'd better get home to the top floor or her grandmother would start getting in a state.

'See you tomorrow,' Nell whispered as the lift came whining and groaning down the shaft to the ground floor. 'Isn't it going to be an exciting time?'

It looked like being so exciting that Sammy couldn't sleep for a long time and then just as he dropped off he remembered Nell chanting, 'The lion and the unicorn were fighting for the crown . . .' And that seemed to make everything quite clear and safe so he fell asleep instantly with no more bother.

In the morning Sammy got into slight trouble from his aunt for letting the grand-daughter of a tenant find out about Uncle Ted's livestock, but this was forgotten in a flash when Uncle Ted himself came leaping down the stairs to the basement two at a time and grabbed the telephone, saying in a husky voice; 'You'll never credit what's happened. Hallo, operator? Give me the police please . . .'

'What?' asked Aunt Jess, going quite pale, 'nobody's been hurt have they?'

Sammy didn't say anything at all as a hideous sinking sensation in his stomach was telling him all too plainly what the fuss was about.

'It's the Unicorn statue,' said Uncle Ted, 'it's vanished.'

'Nonsense,' Aunt Jess shook her head, all the colour coming back into her cheeks, 'Statues don't just disappear. It'd be far too heavy for thieves to carry away.'

'Thieves? Hooligans more like. Oh, sorry officer,' Uncle Ted's tone of voice altered and he began to speak into the phone while Aunt Jess and Sammy watched him. The policeman, it soon became obvious, took much the same view as Aunt Jess about statues doing vanishing acts, and Uncle Ted grew quite heated before he managed to convince the Law that he was not trying to be funny. While all this was going on Sammy managed to edge backwards out of the door and as he tip-toed out of the flat he was nearly sent flying by Nell, who was clutching an enormous shopping basket.

'It was Mr D.,' Nell said instantly, before Sammy could even get his mouth open. 'Granny and me were just washing up when we heard this shout and so we went to see what was happening and Mr D. was practically falling out of the landing window pointing at the Unicorn, I mean where the Unicorn used to be, and his eyes were absolutely bulging. It was quite funny really, only a bit scaring too. Granny gave him a whack on his arm with her stick and told him to pull himself together and to say what the trouble was.

She didn't believe him at first ...'

'Nobody believes it at first. Nobody ever will,' said Sammy, a truly prophetic remark as not one single person who was told the story of the vanishing statue thought it was anything but a joke to begin with.

'Then Mr D. saw your Uncle Ted and I said I'd do the shopping, because it was an excuse to come down and see you. What are we going to do?'

'Keep our mouths shut for a start and think. I looked up Elysian Fields in the encyclopedia this morning, but it's no help. It doesn't seem to be a real place at all. It's supposed to be the land of perfect happiness ruled over by Rhada somebody. The Greeks made it up. The Ancient Greeks—you *know*.'

'Like in History?' Nell asked doubtfully.

'Yup. Oh crikey, listen ...'

There was the familiar wail of a police siren and a sleek black car drew up outside the back entrance to the flats and three policemen got out. The fore-shortened figures of Uncle Ted and Mr D. closely followed by a number of the tenants and a growing band of passers-by gathered round and there was much pointing and shaking of heads and then, as though an invisible cord had been pulled, every single person in the crowd turned to look at the Gardens. Uncle Ted produced a key and led the way, closely followed by the figures of Mr D., the policemen and as many of the crowd who were quick enough to slip through the gate before it was slammed and locked.

Uncle Ted and his companions came to a halt before the mound of marble fragments and one of the policemen knelt down and picked up a piece and stared at it as though it was solid gold at least. Mr D. was fairly dancing from foot to foot in his agitation and Uncle Ted just stood there shaking his head slowly from side to side.

'Got it,' said Sammy, making a hideous face because he was thinking so hard. 'Come on, quick.' And he gripped Nell's hand and pulled her down the stairs to the basement by which time she was too breathless to ask any questions.

'Got to move the animals,' Sammy said, 'put 'em in with the Unicorn. It won't like it much, but it can't be helped.'

'But why?'

'Can't explain now, no time. Gently now . . .'

Of course, no matter how carefully they went the enormous cage got rocked around quite a bit and the birds protested furiously, screeching and flying backwards and forwards inside their moving home. Sammy took down the key to the coal house and gripped it between his teeth and somehow, panting and muttering, he and Nell managed to get the birds out of the dark side entrance of the flat and down the gloomy passage to the Unicorn.

The creature surveyed Sammy and Nell in its usual dreamy manner.

'How kind,' it said, flicking back a lock of its flowing mane so that it swung round the creature's single horn in a glossy white curl. 'You have brought me some company . . .'

'We'll be back with a lot more in half a jiff,' Sammy promised and dragged Nell away to the flat for the turtles. Their home, while not nearly as large as the cage, was a great deal heavier and a considerable amount of water had to be bailed down the kitchen sink before the tank could be moved. By the time the goldfish too had been transported to their new abode Sammy and Nell were extremely damp, very red in the face and panting hard.

'Can't stop yet,' said Sammy, wiping his arm across his sweaty forehead, 'got to write a note to Uncle Ted to tell him what we've done. If he comes back here with the police and finds his pets have vanished as well as the unicorn he'd probably have a fit!'

Nell laughed at the thought of poor Uncle Ted being faced with yet another disappearing act and Sammy grinned and stopped writing long enough to say.

'Don't worry, I'll hang on to the coal house key. Now you go and do your shopping at Boofers Supermarket and see if you can have a word with Aunty Jess. She works on one of the tills. Tell her—tell her the flat's O.K. if anybody drops in. Only do it carefully, we don't want any more trouble than we've got . . .'

As the policeman on the garden gate flatly refused to allow Sammy to enter, Sammy was very glad that he had written such a cautious note to his Uncle just in case anybody else should happen to read it. All the scrap of paper said was. 'Home is tidy for visitors, O.K. Sammy.' When this had been passed on to Uncle Ted and he had waved his thanks, Sammy was given permission to join the group round the remains of the Unicorn's plinth. The group had grown considerably as there were now two men taking photographs, three men with notebooks asking questions and more policemen than previously.

The excitement of the missing unicorn lasted all day and there were headlines in the evening papers one of which said, 'Famous Statue Stolen', and the other 'Theft of Famous Statue'. This also had a somewhat blurred photograph of Uncle Ted looking extremely surprised with a scowling Mr Dimitriadi at his side. Both newspapers had quite long articles about the disappearance and there was even a brief reference to it on the television news.

'Fame at *last!*' said Aunty Jess in a low voice as she washed up the supper things. She had to speak like that as Uncle Ted was still talking to a policeman in the front room. 'Oh Sammy dear, it was clever of you to think of moving the animals. I do hope they'll be all right out there in the shed, poor things.'

'I'll just go and have a look to make quite sure . . .' said Sammy and slipped away.

'Well?' the Unicorn said, 'What progress have you made?'

'I like that,' Sammy replied, 'when Nell and I've had an awful day just keeping you safe from whatever it is you're afraid of. It's not the police is it?'

'Oh dear no,' the Unicorn gave a soft braying sound which could have been a laugh. 'No, those who would capture me are against all law and order. As I am White Magic, so They are Black. They would capture and kill me for my horn.'

The creature spoke quite calmly for it was used to being hunted and took it all as a matter of course, but it made Sammy shiver and when there was a faint knock on the door he nearly leapt out of his skin.

'It's only me,' came Nell's whisper.

Sammy let her in and she went over to the Unicorn and stroked its chilly, glossy neck, murmuring in its ear.

'Do you know who they are, these enemies of yours?' asked Sammy.

'No,' the Unicorn didn't even seem particularly interested as it arched its neck, caught sight of itself in the speckly glass and came as near to a smile as a Unicorn can. 'Well, what are you going to do now?'

'Find somebody else who might help,' said Sammy,

who had been turning this over and over in his mind all day. 'What about the lion?'

The Unicorn snorted, tossed its head and turned a complete circle.

'Oh *him*,' it said, 'that mangy animal. I suppose he *might*, just for old time's sake. Is he still about then?'

'I don't know about THE lion,' Sammy replied truthfully, 'I think there are lots and lots of lions. They're not like you.'

'Agreed.'

'And the nearest lions I can think of are at the Zoo. But I don't know how to speak to a lion.'

'Yes, they are a bit stupid. Never mind, I'll do all the talking.'

'But we couldn't get you into the zoo. We couldn't even get you down the Earls Court Road without everybody going mad.'

'What a terrible fusser you are,' the Unicorn said unfairly. 'If that's all that's worrying you I can soon arrange it perfectly well. Kindly draw the name of the place to which we are going on the ground.'

'Go on,' urged Nell as Sammy continued to sit motionless, gaping at the Unicorn. 'Oh well if you won't I will,' and she pulled an end of coloured chalk out of her pocket and got down on her hands and knees and wrote the words LONDON ZOO, and then added REGENTS PARK. And then between the 'Zoo' and the 'Regents', LIONS' CAGE, PLEASE, just to make everything perfectly plain.

'Now then, look here,' said Sammy, who was still staring at the Unicorn, 'we just can't go to the zoo like anybody else. I mean *we* could but *you* can't—and anyway,' he finished triumphantly, 'It's past closing time, so there.'

'Just as well I should have thought,' replied the

Unicorn, 'as you are so anxious to avoid being seen with me. I find that rather hard to bear, however never mind,' and it snorted softly, tossing up its head.

'It's not that at all,' shouted Sammy so loudly that the budgerigars woke up underneath their blanket and shouted back. He added more softly, 'Don't you understand—we can't *get* you there. A taxi'd cost about a pound I should think and anyway I don't believe you can take Unicorns in taxis. Why I'm not even sure that they take ...'

Sammy was about to say 'dogs', but luckily stopped in the nick of time as he suddenly realised that the Unicorn really *would* take offence if he compared it to a dog. It appeared to be a very touchy creature.

'Taxis, taxis,' the Unicorn said, once again restored to good humour by this ridiculous notion. 'Who said anything about *taxis? I* shall take you. It's a great honour, but then I'm sure you're *fully* aware of that. Up you get and gently please. I'm extremely strong, yet delicate at the same time. Up, up, up!'

There was a note in the creature's husky, echoing voice that said quite clearly, 'Oh for goodness sake *do as you're told.*' It was a note with which Sammy and Nell were very familiar and although they both wanted to ask a great many more questions they obeyed it automatically, and the pair of them slithered cautiously onto the Unicorn's smooth and chilly back and even as they did so the Unicorn beat out a tattoo with its sharp front hooves, rocked its head up and down and muttered quickly under its breath all at the same time.

The coal house swam dizzily and turned from shadowy grey to blinding white and the sleepy, indignant chatter of the budgerigars died away and Nell and Sammy hung on for dear life and shut their eyes so tightly that in each case they quite distinctly saw a perfect firework display of coloured stars. And then these too vanished and there was a rushing sound like the wind, the slightest of jolts and then a very different kind of sound indeed. A sound such as an extremely large cat might make when it was woken up from a comfortable sleep and wasn't too happy about it. Only it would have to be a cat about four times the size of the usual variety and as he heard this sound Sammy stopped feeling sick and giddy and became almost as cold as the Unicorn itself.

He very, very slowly opened one reluctant eye and with a hand that trembled violently he pulled Nell off the back of the Unicorn as he slid down himself.

'What is it?' whispered Nell, who was not prepared to open her eyes for anyone or anything at the present moment.

'What did you write on the floor?' Sammy asked in a husky croak.

Nell told him and then, like Sammy, she suddenly realised just exactly what she HAD written.

'The-the-the l-l-lions' cage,' said Nell in a squeak.

'Right, bang inside it,' agreed Sammy and felt his bones turn to water as he saw, in the starlight, the great shadowy shape of the disturbed lion come padding towards them while at the same time the Unicorn put down its head and letting out a shrill cry prepared to charge.

'AAAAAAAAARA,' growled the lion, its eyes yellow as agate and it tightened its muscles for a split second and then launched itself into the air in a great leap at its traditional enemy.

5. *The O Pear Girl*

There are sometimes moments which are so terrifying that you just don't feel frightened at all. You're quite sure that this awful thing cannot possibly be happening to you and that really you are standing to one side and watching it all take place with somebody else. Which was just the way that Sammy and Nell now felt as they stood side by side, their eyes and mouths wide open, their four feet planted as heavily as four lumps of lead on the floor of the lion's cage.

'EEEEEEEEEE,' the Unicorn repeated its shrill cry, waving its head slightly, rather like a cobra about to strike, its long pointed horn aiming for the centre of the lion's body.

'It is, it's going to—oh it can't, it can't...' whispered Sammy at the same moment and added, 'Don't look, don't look . . .'

But they could neither of them shut their eyes and then at the very very last split second in time both creatures swerved a fraction and the lion twisted sideways in the air, exactly as a cat does when it changes its mind, and landed with a soft thud to one side of the Unicorn, which tossed up its head and skitted round and round on its delicate hooves. Once again the pair of them took up battle positions, their eyes fixed on each other as they manoeuvred for the best place from which to attack.

Nell gave a little moan, her hands gripping Sammy's arm so tightly that his fingers began to get pins and needles.

'Stop them, stop them,' she whispered from between chattering teeth. As Sammy was less than half their respective sizes it was extremely unlikely that he would be able to do any such thing, but he did manage to say.

'Please, please don't.'

Which was very brave under the circumstances as it might have drawn attention to himself. However, neither creature took the slightest notice and they continued to circle each other, the lion growling deep inside its shaggy throat while the Unicorn uttered its shrill cry. Suddenly they froze into stillness and then the leap and the waving of the horn were repeated and yet again they somehow managed to avoid touching each other by a hair's breadth. It was when all this feinting, charging and jumping had been done several times that Sammy drew a deep breath, shook his arm free from Nell and said shakily.

'It's all right, you idiot. They're not going to hurt each other. They're playing, can't you see?'

Nell sank slowly down to the floor of the cage where she sat with her legs straight out in front of her and her mouth wide open, while Sammy rubbed his fingers to get rid of the cramp and tried to make his brain think of a way out of the situation. Being transported from the best coal house at Leo Mansions to *inside* a lion's cage at Regents Park Zoo in a matter of seconds really took quite a lot of getting used to, let alone witnessing a mock battle.

Then as suddenly as it had started it was all over and the lion thudded down, rolled over and over and then lay on its back with all four large paws in the air. The Unicorn trotted over to it, put one front hoof lightly on the heaving stomach and raised the other, throwing back its head and standing perfectly motionless. After several seconds of silence broken only by the heavy panting of the lion, the Unicorn rolled one eye in Sammy's direction and looked expectant.

'What?' said Sammy, and then added hurriedly, 'Oh, well done. Jolly good. Congratulations. You've—um—won!'

He gave Nell a slight nudge with his foot and she said like an echo:

'Congratulations. You've won.'

'Applause, applause, applause,' the Unicorn said softly and removed its hoof. 'Actually it was no contest at all. He doesn't even begin to know the rules of the game, let alone the moves. I suppose they don't bother to learn them these days. It's no fun jousting with an amateur, because there's no skill in it. Get up, get up, do.'

The lion obediently did as it was told, shook itself violently and then crouched down with its great head on its front paws. It looked majestic, yet humble at the same time and Nell, who was very fond of all animals, came out of her trance-like state and scrambled to her feet and went over to it and smoothed back the tumbled mane.

'I'm sure you did your best,' she said gently.

The lion turned its head to look up at her, sighed and sank its chin once again on its paws.

'I say, careful,' Sammy exclaimed.

'Oh you needn't worry,' the Unicorn said disdainfully. 'He knows that he's more than met his match, poor old thing. Well, to business although I really don't hold out much hope.'

It beckoned to the lion with its horn and the pair of them went over to one side of the cage and had a long whispered conversation during which the Unicorn snorted several times and the lion's tail drooped and even its mane appeared to grow flatter.

'Just as I thought,' the Unicorn said over its shoulder. 'He says he's never heard of my Elysian Fields. The only fields with which he appears to have even a nodding acquaintance are called Smith, and they sound perfectly disgusting as it's where his meals are bought. Well, there's really nothing to be gained in hanging about here any longer. You'll have to do better next time, you know. You can't expect *me* to be brought out on a wild swan's chase every day of the week.'

'Wild goose,' said Sammy. He was really rather

angry, what with being scared half to death and then told off in this way. 'Goose, goose, goose!'

'Farmyard birds,' the Unicorn replied lightly. 'We don't mix.'

The truth of the matter was that the Unicorn too was suffering from shock. It had, after all, been a statue for a long while, during which time there had been no opportunity at all for it to keep up its magic, added to which it had just taken part in a traditional mock battle for which it was sadly out of training and the lion, even though a complete amateur, had put up a better show than the Unicorn had expected. Its victory had been quite hardly won and this had touched its most vulnerable point, its pride. Usually exquisitely polite it now let its manner slip still more as it added:

'Indeed the company in which I've recently found myself is not at all what I have been accustomed to.'

The Unicorn was actually referring to the lion, which was now slinking off to its sleeping quarters with its head and tail well down. But Sammy thought it was a direct reference to himself and so, at that moment, a deep and most unfortunate rift opened between him and the Unicorn.

Nell, who had suddenly started to feel overpoweringly sleepy, sensed what was happening in a muddled kind of way and tried to make things better by saying quickly, 'Never mind, beautiful Unicorn, we will find your home for you soon and then everything will be all right. Only please can we go back now, because Granny might start wondering where I am?'

'Certainly.'

Sammy didn't say anything at all, but climbed onto the cold, quivering back with his chin thrust out and a deep determination inside himself that from now on the Unicorn could jolly well look after itself. He was feeling just as obstinate when the giddy, breath-taking journey to Earls Court was over and the three of them were once again in the best coal house.

'Goodnight, dear Unicorn,' said Nell, rather pale and shaky and extremely glad to be back on familiar ground. 'It was—it was very *interesting*.'

'I only wish you could have seen me joust with a lion more worthy of my skill. However, it was not to be. Please would you wipe out those words of command?'

Nell did as she was asked, but unfortunately owing to tiredness she didn't do it very well. Sammy said nothing at all, but stumped about making quite sure that the birds, fish and turtles were all right and then without a backward glance led the way out of the coal house and locked the door.

'What's the matter?' Nell asked timidly.

'Nothing,' said Sammy untruthfully, 'nothing at all. Goodnight. Well, if it thinks I'm going to help it now it's very much mistaken. It's quite wrong,' he added so as to make his meaning perfectly clear, 'because I'm not going to. If *you* want to, all right go ahead. Showing off like that and then calling me a—a farm-yard person.'

'I think it meant the goose, but . . .'

'Ha!' said Sammy, who had now really worked himself up into a rage and somewhat unfairly decided to direct it at Nell. 'Ha! Ha! HA! If you want to go looking for those silly Elysian Fields—and they don't even exist—you jolly well go right ahead. I don't care. I don't even care if the Black Magic lot win. It'd serve it right. Here.'

And Sammy thrust the key into Nell's surprised hand and went off down the passage looking, in fact, every bit as proud and disdainful as the Unicorn and leaving a very astonished Nell staring after him.

Anger doesn't last long and even if you have a good reason for it, as Sammy did have in a way, it tends to vanish after you have thought things over. Added to which Sammy was a very fair-minded boy so that by the next day he had simmered down quite considerably. However he had a certain amount of pride and when he woke up the following morning and realised that he'd have to go and ask Nell for the key back—somebody had to see to Uncle Ted's pets after all—it took him quite a long time to decide to go up to the top floor. It was Uncle Ted's day for cleaning down the stairs, too, which meant that Sammy couldn't take the lift, so he stumped upwards passing his Uncle and had just rather breathlessly reached the top floor when the door of Number 23 opened and the 'O Pear' girl came out. She looked both startled and a bit scared when she saw Sammy and then to his surprise she said softly, 'I wonder, could you spare a minute please?'

'If something's gone wrong with the central heating or the water you want Uncle Ted, I mean Mr Jenkins the caretaker,' Sammy said ungraciously.

'Oh no, no. It is you I wish to speak to.'

The O Pear girl smiled nervously and held open the door of the flat and Sammy, still scowling, walked in. The only other occasions on which tenants had invited him in were once to a party at which Sammy had found himself to be the oldest by years and years, and secondly when a very cross lady on the second floor had accused him of making a noise on the landing. But on this occasion there was no sound at all except for the gentle crowings of a baby and the O Pear girl didn't seem angry but only uneasy.

'I am sorry to ask you,' she said. 'Please forgive my English which is not very good, but I think you could help me. Why did the policemen come yesterday? Has some person done something wrong? Yes?'

'Oh that. No, it was the Unicorn. The Unicorn statue you know. It vanished. Went . . .' Sammy waved his arms as the girl looked at him blankly. 'Down there. Gone.' And he went over to the window and pointed.

'Oh, oh, oh,' the O Pear girl sat down and added, 'Is gone far, please?'

Sammy opened his mouth to tell her that it had hardly gone any distance at all and then quickly changed his mind, as all the Unicorn's vague references to Black Magic came back to him. She didn't look a very frightening person, in fact quite the opposite, but it might be wise to be discreet.

'Why?' he asked. 'Why are you interested?'

'It was so beautiful. Every day I take the baby of whom I have the care, to look at it. I am a Greek and we very much admire the Unicorn in my country. To us it is a creature of great power. I have a H'uncle living in London and many times I have told him about the handsome statue in the Gardens. He wished to see it and I had promised that one day I would bring him here to—to admire the Unicorn.'

Sammy didn't know what to say. The O Pear girl seemed nice enough, but all the same you couldn't be too careful and he wasn't at all sure that he could trust her.

'Well, it may turn up again,' he said weakly, 'a lot of people think that it was destroyed . . . broken into pieces you know . . . by the storm the other night. I mean nobody'd steal a statue, would they?'

'Some people might wish to do so. Bad people.'

There was a long rather awkward silence which was broken by Sammy saying, 'Where does your Huncle, I mean your uncle, live?'

'Chepstow Villas. He has a shop down the Portobello Market. He sells many things. His name is Mr Rhadaman. One day perhaps you will meet him. Yes?'

The name Rhadaman stirred some distant memory in Sammy's mind and he said cheerfully, 'Oh yes, rather. I go down the Porto sometimes with Uncle Ted and Aunty Jess. It's quite fun.'

The O Pear girl talked a bit about the market and then the baby started crying and she showed Sammy out of the flat and closed the door behind him. He had a funny feeling that there were a lot of other things she would have liked to ask him but, even though she didn't seem to be a real grown-up person in a way, he hadn't felt quite at ease with her either, so he was glad to get away although he was a bit worried.

It was all very unsatisfactory somehow and Sammy was still turning it over in his mind when he rang the doorbell of Number 21. Somewhere he felt he had been given a clue, but he wasn't sure what it was.

Old Mrs Bates opened the door and leaning on her stick said, 'Hallo Sammy. What do you want?'

'Nell.'

'But she went down to see you quite a long time ago, dear.'

'To see me?' Sammy repeated. 'But . . .'

'There's nothing wrong is there, dear?'

'Oh no,' Sammy replied. 'Nothing at all. We must've passed each other. Thank you . . .'

Sammy turned and started to run down the stairs, unaware that Mr Dimitriadi had appeared at his own front door, his dark eyes gleaming. Down and down

Sammy ran and round and round until he reached the basement flat and let himself out of the side door. But long before he reached the coal house he knew inside himself what he would find.

There were the budgerigars, the turtles and the fish all right, but that was all. Of Nell and the Unicorn there was no trace at all except for a somewhat blurred message in chalk on the floor.

'Nell,' Sammy said, 'Unicorn—where are you?'

But there was no answer at all except for the busy chirping of the budgerigars as they flew backwards and forwards across their cage.

6. Unicorn House

Nell had woken up early and very full of beans after a good night's sleep. She remembered how silly Sammy had been after the adventure of last night and how he and the Unicorn had very nearly quarrelled. What they really needed was a person who could sort out everything with no trouble at all and it had nothing to do with Lions or Black Magic or stuff like that. Boys—and Unicorns come to that—just didn't know where to look!

Nell got out of bed and pulled on her quilted dressing-gown and skipped down the passage to where the telephone and its directories were kept. She picked out the volume marked S-Z and ran her finger down the page.

And there it was, quite plain for anyone to see too! Unicorn House, London E.C.3. Well if the people there couldn't help, who could! And Nell, with a very satisfied smile on her face, marched into the kitchen and put on the kettle for breakfast. As it slowly came to the boil she got dressed, washed her face, cleaned her teeth and brushed her hair and smiled at herself in the mirror. It was all so perfectly simple!

Thirty minutes later the Unicorn came out of a light doze—it was more tired than it cared to admit even to itself—to find a sunny-faced Nell sweeping the blankets off the birds' cage.

'*Good* morning,' said Nell.

''Morning.'

'Have you slept well?'

'I never sleep,' the Unicorn replied, quite untruthfully.

'Good. I've found the people who can help you.'

'Where's Sammy?' the Unicorn asked uneasily. It liked Eleanor, she appreciated him and understood his feelings, but Sammy, although bad tempered and unreasonable, was somehow very reliable in his way.

'Oh I expect he'll be here soon. Now dear beautiful Unicorn, it's all perfectly simple because I've discovered a—a place . . .'

'A Temple of mine?' the Unicorn said, perking up its head.

'Yes. At least I think it is. It must be really because it's called Unicorn House . . .'

'Very right too . . .'

'In E.C.3 . . .'

'What is that?'

'It's a—a part of London. If we go there they *must* know how to find your home. I'm sure they will. Can I get on your back?'

'Not till you've written the magic words. I suppose it is perfectly safe?' the Unicorn added, looking a bit uneasily over its shining white shoulder.

'Safe?' Nell repeated, getting down onto her knees to write the words on the floor, a floor on which the previous chalk marks were not completely wiped out although she was too excited to notice this. 'Safe? Why *you* can't be afraid of anything when you fought the lion so bravely in the Zoo'

'An untrained lion too,' agreed the Unicorn, gazing at its reflection in the speckled glass, 'how very right you are. Write on, oh fair one, write on. You are perfectly correct, the slaves of my temple will aid me. Are the symbols well done?'

'I think so,' Nell replied a shade doubtfully and indeed, although she had written UNICORN HOUSE, LONDON E.C.3, PLEASE as clearly as possible with the piece of chalk which had now shrunk quite considerably, the words were not exactly distinct.

'Up, up,' the Unicorn ordered in its husky, echoing voice, 'onto my back, let us yet again seek the Fields of Elysium . . .'

Nell did as she was told and hung on tightly to the cold, curling mane of the Unicorn. Part of her wished very much that Sammy was here to share this adventure and yet part of her was quite pleased to be doing it all on her own just so that she could show how clever she could be. And then the Unicorn muttered and reared up on its hind legs and there was no time for anything at all except to hang on as the birds, turtles and fish swam round and round in faster and faster circles until there was nothing at all except a great white whirling mass of clouds.

'There,' the Unicorn said breathlessly. All those years of inactivity had taken their toll and it wasn't nearly as fit as it had fondly imagined for as it came to a halt it felt quite distinctly a pull to one side, almost as though it was being tugged by a leading rein. 'There . . .' it repeated, its sides shivering.

Nell, who felt a bit sick at all this fast travelling, opened her eyes, looked about her and then shut them again.

'Where are we?' she asked shakily.

'At—at my temple,' replied the Unicorn in an equally uncertain voice. 'The place at which you inscribed us to be. It is a very *great* place.'

It was indeed for as Nell, most courageously, managed to open both her eyes she saw that they were very nearly up in the clouds. They were, in fact, poised almost in those fleeting shadows on the top of a skyscraper which rose like a cliff above the busy streets so very far below. The people in the streets looked like hurrying ants while the sprawling traffic appeared to be composed of snuffling, bumbling black beetles. Or, in the case of buses, red beetles. It was like looking down the sides of a vertical canyon and Nell, who had never been very good at heights, said shakily, 'I don't like it, I don't like it. Take me away.'

The Unicorn reared up, trying to obey her command, but Nell who had been unprepared for this sudden action, slid sideways and before she could stop herself she slipped clean off its back and landed with a thump on a piece of concrete which, luckily for her, stuck out sideways from the building.

'Help, Unicorn, help,' Nell shouted, hanging on for all she was worth to this rough support.

'I can't, I can't,' the Unicorn replied despairingly as it reared and twisted, shaking its beautiful head, 'something even stronger than myself calls and I must obey. I cannot, oh I cannot . . .'

Nell gripped the concrete on which she was seated astraddle and yelled back.

'You must, you must. Get Sammy . . . oh Unicorn get Sammy . . .'

The Unicorn stopped twisting for a second and turned to look at her.

'I will, I will,' it cried, 'hold on, I shall call my slaves . . . I . . .'

And then to Nell's horror it gave one last convulsive shake, reared up, stood poised against the sky for a second and then became thin and translucent so that the hurrying clouds showed through it—and then vanished completely.

'Unicorn,' Nell shouted, 'Unicorn . . .'

On the twenty-first floor of the Unicorn Building a most important board meeting was in progress. The Chairman of the meeting (it was a board of directors) Mr Box was in the very middle of his speech when he became aware of a great deal of noise above his head. As he knew very well that he was on the top floor of Unicorn House and that therefore there could be nobody above him at all, Mr Box could not at first believe his ears. However the noise continued and, what was far worse, was distracting the attention of the Board so that Mr Box at last had to pause. He glanced along the line of directors, all of whom were now looking towards the ceiling and all of whom had quite obviously become aware of the noise overhead.

'Gentlemen,' said Mr Box and all the heads turned, although a trifle reluctantly, in his direction. 'Gentlemen, we now come to the next point on the agenda, our oil fields in Kuwait, and I would like to draw your attention to . . .'

But as he spoke there came quite clearly from above their heads a voice calling.

'Unicorn . . .'

Even Mr Box was unable to stop himself looking at the ceiling. He took a deep breath and then stared down the long polished table. He said very quietly, 'Perhaps you, Mr Cowgill, would go and see just what is happening?'

Mr Cowgill, a rather pale-faced young man, bowed and left the room. Mr Box took another deep, very deep breath and went on with the meeting.

Within a very few minutes Mr Cowgill, looking even paler than before and very windswept, reappeared somewhat unceremoniously and announced, 'There is a child on the roof. I've re-locked the door.'

'Impossible,' snapped Mr Box. 'However,' and he lifted the telephone at his side and gave a few quick orders. He then turned to the Company Secretary and began to speak to him as a buzz of conversation broke out among the other gentlemen present. One of them, a very old looking gentleman with a long white beard took Mr Cowgill aside and said in a low voice, 'What can a child be doing up there, almost in the sky? Should we not rescue her? She might be in great danger of falling.'

'If she got up there in the first place, then she should be able to get down again,' Mr Cowgill replied crossly. He didn't like heights himself and once he had got up onto the roof everything had seemed very unsafe and uncomfortable and, although he would never admit such a thing to any of the other members of the board, he had felt extremely dizzy and unwell up on the parapet. Now that he was safely back in the boardroom he wasn't at all sure that he believed the evidence of his own eyes as it stood to reason that it was quite impossible for a small girl to be straddling one of their concrete blocks. For a long time now he had felt that he had been overworking . . .

The elderly gentleman looked at him in a very worried way and then tried to push his way through the other gentlemen clustered round Mr Box who was saying, 'Please, please . . . gentlemen, there is no need to feel alarmed. If some person—or persons—' and he looked hard at Mr Cowgill who was sitting slumped in a chair with his eyes closed and small beads of sweat on his forehead, 'or *persons* have somehow managed to gain access to our roof in order to make illicit tape-recordings of our meetings, they will be dealt with very shortly. Our Chief Security Officer and two of his men are now on their way up here.

'Industrial spies,' somebody said angrily, 'really one isn't safe from them anywhere these days and even if these fellows *are* caught . . .'

'There aren't any fellows,' Mr Cowgill said faintly, 'There was only one person on the roof, a child, I keep telling you.'

But nobody paid any attention to him as they were too busy arguing between themselves as to what to do for the best.

'It is a very difficult situation,' said Mr Box, 'And a very delicate one too. If this gang . . .'

'There isn't any gang,' shouted Mr Cowgill, suddenly opening his eyes and thumping his fists on the arm of his chair.

'Pull yourself together, man,' said Mr Box angrily, 'you're thoroughly overwrought, that's your trouble. Now then gentlemen, as we cannot allow any rumours to get out about our future plans for Unicorn Overseas Development we must make some minor alterations. Throw up a smoke screen so to speak so as to confuse our competitors. This gang,' and he glared at the pale and trembling Mr Cowgill, 'this gang, gentlemen, may have been in radio contact with their employers, who may already be in possession of some vital information which has been overheard here this morning. Therefore we must act immediately.'

There was a general nodding of heads and with two exceptions all the gentlemen said, 'Here, here, agreed.'

The two who said nothing at all were the old man with the white silky beard and Mr Cowgill, who now looked as though he was about to burst into tears. He jumped quite violently when the old man sat down beside him and said quietly, 'You are quite sure, are you not, that there is only one person on our roof and that this person is not grown-up?'

'Yes. At least I think I am. I don't know anymore, really I don't. I *thought* I saw a child just sitting there, almost up in the clouds. But it can't be true can it? Not really. The door to the roof was bolted on the inside so she must have come down from the sky and that can only mean one thing. I've lost my reason.'

'Steady, steady my boy,' the old gentleman said in such a kind voice that Mr Cowgill, who as the youngest member of the Board was used to being bullied and put upon by everybody else, or so it often seemed to him, had to pull out a large white handkerchief to blow his nose.

'Yes, yes,' said the old gentleman, 'now then describe this little one to me.'

'She had a green face and three eyes,' said Mr Cowgill and laughed in such a strange way that everybody else stopped talking and looked at him and a sudden hush descended on the entire room. Even the portraits round the walls appeared to be frowning at him, while Mr Box's frown was the worst of all. 'No, she didn't,' gabbled Mr Cowgill getting somewhat unsteadily to his feet. 'She was a perfectly ordinary child with long dark hair and she was wearing a blue jumper and blue trousers. So there!'

'Oh yes,' said Mr Box, 'I see,' and he laughed too but in a way which made it perfectly plain that he didn't believe a word of all this. 'Well, in that case my dear Cowgill, in—that—case, why did you not merely take her by the arm and bring her down here so that we could all meet the young lady. Hm?'

'Because,' shouted Mr Cowgill and then stopped as he suddenly realised why he had done no such thing. He had felt so sick and dizzy and really extremely unwell twenty-two storeys above the City that his only passionate desire had been to clamber back to the safety of having four stout walls between himself and that terrible drop of hundreds and hundreds of feet to the ground below. He took a deep breath and looked at all the half-smiling faces and then step by step he retreated towards the door of the board room until his fingers found the knob and turned it. 'Because I'm a coward, that's why,' he said in such a strange tone of voice that several of the important gentlemen present felt chilly shivers run down their respectable backs. 'But I'll show you all!'

And before anybody could stop him Mr Cowgill

had slipped through the now half-open door, slammed it behind him and vanished. Nobody else moved for at least ten seconds and then three of the younger men present rushed forwards, only to be stopped by the smooth, commanding voice of Mr Box as he said, 'Let him go, let him go, gentlemen. Cowgill is obviously in the grip of a nervous breakdown, poor fellow. And anyway he won't get far or do any harm. Mr Black, our trustworthy Chief Security Officer, has the entire building ringed by this time and his delay in arriving here may well be due to the fact that he . . .' Mr Box paused and smiled benignly, 'he thought it wise that he and his men should call in at our Top Defence Section en route.'

'You mean . . .' said the white bearded gentleman in a horrified voice. 'You mean . . .?'

'Exactly Mr Rhadaman. Our guards will be armed!' said Mr Box triumphantly. 'Armed!'

7. *Mr Cowgill to the Rescue*

Nell had been sitting for so long with her eyes tight shut and her hands and knees gripping the concrete support that she had no idea how much time had passed since the Unicorn had vanished. Nobody can go on being really frightened for ever and after a bit a kind of dreamy something-will-happen-to-make-it-all-right sensation had stolen over her, besides which at the back of her mind she was quite certain that the Unicorn would not desert her for ever and nor would Sammy. Between the two of them they were bound to work out a plan of escape so all *she* had to do was to hang on until they arrived. So when a voice said hoarsely, 'Hey, psst, you.'

Nell replied without bothering to open her eyes. 'Is that you, Unicorn?'

'No, it's me, Cowgill,' said Mr Cowgill.

'Oh!' said Nell and opened her eyes, which was a dreadful mistake because she immediately became aware that she was on the edge of a terrible empty space and at once her hands became all sweaty and she started to feel sick.

'Ohhhhhh,' said Nell and swayed.

'Don't,' implored Mr Cowgill. His face was just as green as Nell's was now becoming and like her his forehead and hands were getting wet and slippery. He had always been frightened of heights and as he shut and bolted the door behind him he had the awful feeling that the whole of the top of the Unicorn Building was dipping and swaying so that at any moment he would roll over the edge of it. He knew, deep inside himself that this was nonsense, but all the same the only sensible thing to do was to get down on his hands and knees and to start crawling towards the small figure on the skyline. He had never before been quite so frightened as he was now, but he kept on shuffling forwards as he said, 'Please don't look. Whatever you do, don't look down. I'm very glad you're real though. You are real, aren't you?'

'Oh yes,' said Nell in a very faint voice. 'I'm perfectly real.'

'What's your name?' asked Mr Cowgill, pausing for a second to wipe his dark-suited arm across his eyes.

'Eleanor Margaret Bates and I think I'm going to be sick.'

'No, you're not. Hold on just a little more and I'll rescue you, Eleanor Margaret Bates and . . .' Mr Cowgill had to stop because like Nell he was feeling extremely unwell and the sky now seemed to be whirling round and round his head in horrible echoing circles as he reached the parapet. He took one hand off the concrete roof and pushed it against his mouth and shook his head and then somehow he managed to go on, 'and then you can tell me all about this Unicorn.'

'I think you'd better hurry up,' said Nell, 'because I feel a bit funny.'

'I'm coming,' said Mr Cowgill, 'I'm coming as fast as I can, Eleanor,' and with a truly heroic effort he reached out one trembling hand towards the small figure who was swaying against the whirling blue circle of the sky . . .

And at exactly the same moment Sammy was saying in an equally shaky voice.

'Where have you *been*? Where's Nell? What's happened?'

'One question at a time,' the Unicorn replied faintly. It was shivering and shaking and for once it looked far from beautiful with its white mane hanging in grey dull streaks and its sides heaving. 'Oh, if you only knew what I've been through. They nearly got me this time. They were after me, I could feel them pulling and pulling. I had to fight with all my strength. Oh dear, oh dear . . .' And it snorted violently as it sank to its knees in the best coal house.

'Never mind about that now,' said Sammy, whose own face in the gloom was nearly as white as that of the Unicorn. 'What's happened to Nell? Where did you take her? Oh do get up!'

Sammy had spent a very nerve-racking half-hour waiting for some kind of news and he had quite forgotten that only a few hours ago he had sworn to himself to have nothing more to do with the Unicorn. But the disappearance of Eleanor coupled with the creature's woe-begone appearance had made all that seem silly and pointless.

The Unicorn made an effort to pull itself together and scrambled to its hooves in a somewhat ungainly way which only showed just how upset it was as it normally did everything so gracefully.

'She said she had found the way to my temple,' it said shakily, 'and I took her to this place in Easythree.'

'In *what*?'

'That is what she told me. Easythree. Here, it is inscribed upon the ground. Perhaps it is one of your modern magic symbols?'

'I don't think we have any really. Let me look. Oh move over, do.'

'Doing my best,' said the Unicorn in a hurt voice as it backed up against the fish tank so that a perfect scurry of fish activity then took place. 'They were very close to me, the Black Magic ones, I could sense them. As soon as we came down on that place I felt them all round me—I'm very sensitive you know—and then quite suddenly there was this Pull. I tried to withstand it, I fought and fought and Eleanor was crying for my aid. Oh it was all most distressing. I am *exhausted*.'

'What do you mean, crying for your aid. Is she in danger?'

Sammy sounded so fierce that the Unicorn sheered away and knocked into the aviary, its great round eyes rolling so that it looked perfectly demented.

'I was in danger,' it said, snorting heavily. 'I. I who am the last Unicorn. There is only one of me. I must be protected at all costs . . . oh!'

The Unicorn stopped speaking abruptly as Sammy got up off his knees and walked towards it. He was usually a peace-minded boy who didn't get into fights unless he had to, but at this very minute he was so angry that he really looked quite fierce and frightening.

'Shut up,' Sammy said, 'shut up about yourself for once and think about somebody else. Nell's been jolly kind to you and now it's your turn to help *her*. All I can read on the floor is Unicorn House and then some letters, only they're all mixed up with that zoo message bit. Now come on, jolly well remember, WHERE DID YOU TAKE HER!' and Sammy actually gripped the Unicorn by its white mane and shook it.

'I'm tired,' quavered the Unicorn. 'I've been on one journey and . . .'

'I'll write, "Black Magic Lot come and get me", on the floor,' threatened Sammy. The Unicorn snorted, threw its head about and then said sulkily:

'You'll be the death of me. Well, as far as I can recall we went to this temple of mine, Unicorn House, Easythree. I'm not sure I can make the return journey though . . .'

'Oh yes you will,' said Sammy and plonked down on his knees again and with the end of the chalk which Nell had dropped he re-chalked over Nell's letters as best he could and then swung himself onto the Unicorn's quivering back, and nudged it with his heels.

Even as he did so the door which gave onto the roof of Unicorn House shook and shivered and a voice said, 'Stand back, we're going to fire!'

Nell and Mr Cowgill looked at each other. They were both on all-fours and Mr Cowgill was gripping her wrists painfully as Nell said quaveringly.

'Who's that?'

'The Chief Security Officer, Mr Black.'

'What will he do?'

'I don't know. You'll be all right because you're a child. They've got nothing against you, but as for me . . .' and Mr Cowgill laughed rather wildly. 'They'll probably lock me up. They think I'm mad and perhaps I am. I've been overworking for years and years because I wanted to get on the Board, but now it all seems pointless, pointless.'

'Oh, don't, please don't,' Nell said, 'You rescued me and that was terribly brave. Just about the bravest thing in the whole world when you get so ill being up high. I might have fallen right over the edge if you hadn't pulled me back, so you saved my life. Just wait till I tell my grandmother what you did, why you should get a medal.'

'They won't give me any medal, they'll probably put me away. How *did* you get up here?'

'I told you. The Unicorn brought me.'

'Better not tell *Them* that or they'll lock you up too,' said Mr Cowgill, who was suffering from a violent reaction and was now quite determined to look on the dark side of the situation, 'this may be Unicorn House, but . . .'

And then he stopped as two things happened simultaneously. There was a tremendous noise, bang-bang-bang and at the same time a spinning shadow appeared out of the clouds and then came to rest with a delicate tip-tip-tip beside them. The shadow became more solid, stopped spinning and transformed itself into a somewhat breathless snow white pony with one long horn in the centre of its forehead and on whose back was a very anxious-looking boy with his hair up on end.

Mr Cowgill surveyed this somewhat startling apparition in a surprisingly calm manner.

'There,' he said in a satisfied voice, 'I knew it would happen and it has. I've gone quite, quite barmy and in a way I have to admit it *is* a relief. My doctor told me some months ago that I was heading for trouble, and I must say I rather dreaded what might happen, but this is really rather pleasant as I'd anticipated something far more nasty. This, I presume, is the Unicorn of which you spoke?'

'That's right,' agreed Nell, who had now wound both arms round the Unicorn's trembling neck and was smoothing back its tousled mane, 'don't you think it's beautiful?'

'Very beautiful,' agreed Mr Cowgill dreamily, a remark which drew a small pleased snort and toss of the head from the creature in question.

Sammy, however, was in no mood for any exchange of pleasantries. He had experienced the usual upside-down feeling of a Unicorn journey, he had only the faintest idea of his whereabouts and although he was almost overwhelmingly glad to see that Nell was safe and sound he didn't know the man who was staring at the Unicorn in a very odd, bemused fashion and he had a very powerful feeling that Trouble was not far away. And indeed even as he tried to work out exactly what was going on a funny looking door on the roof burst open and a man wearing a kind of crash helmet and overalls appeared. Behind him were two other men in similar garb and behind *them* were a whole crowd of faces.

'Hands up!' ordered the man in the doorway and jerked something which looked remarkably like a gun.

'Is that a lance?' asked the Unicorn with deep interest. 'If it is, it's very short. I shouldn't think it would be any use at all.'

'No, no,' said Mr Cowgill calmly, 'lances went out of use hundreds of years ago you know, before gunpowder was invented, I believe. It's probably a gun or maybe a canister of gas. It's Mr Black, our Chief Security Officer.'

'Hands up, I said,' repeated the man. He was staring at the Unicorn, his black eyebrows drawn together in a frown. He looked neither surprised nor bewildered at the scene before him as he slowly advanced towards the quartet on the edge of the roof and it was Sammy who suddenly shattered the strange calm by shouting.

'He's bad—bad—Black—don't you see!'

The Unicorn reared sideways, blowing furiously through its carved nostrils, its mane flying in the stiff breeze and Eleanor cried out.

'No, no it can't be . . .'

'It is, it is,' Sammy replied and grabbed her arm with one hand and the Unicorn's waving mane with the other.

'Black's my name,' the man said softly as he moved forwards another couple of steps, 'and I've got you now, haven't I?' He raised his hand slightly, his eyes fixed on the rearing, circling figure of the prancing Unicorn and at the same moment Mr Cowgill shouted, 'Behind you, look behind you, Black . . .'

The man turned instinctively and Mr Cowgill launched himself across the roof in a flying tackle. There was a tremendous thud and the Chief Security Guard was sent hurtling backwards and into his two assistants, who in turn collided with the members of the Board who had clambered up the narrow stairs to the roof to watch the fun. There was a whole series of thuds and cries and the Chief Security Officer, his arms waving wildly, fell heavily on top of the pile.

'To me, to me,' cried the Unicorn shrilly.

'I am,' Nell replied, scrambling onto its back, 'Oh Sammy hurry . . .'

Sammy half scrambled up onto the Unicorn's trembling back and then slid off again and darted across the roof and seized the breathless Mr Cowgill by the sleeve and yanked him to his feet and pushed him across the concrete blocks and somehow managed to shove him onto the Unicorn.

'I can't, I can't . . .' the Unicorn snorted.

'He jolly well saved you and you must,' Sammy ordered, his own breath coming in great gasps as he somehow managed to pull himself up onto the creature's haunches. 'Home—and sanctuary . . .'

And Sammy looked over his shoulder just in time to see the Chief Security Officer come panting up the stairs with a most terrible expression on his face as with one arm held across his chest as a support he raised his weapon to fire. And then the clear blue sky and the low wisps of white cloud were whirling round and round their heads and all Sammy could do was to hang on as hard as he could so as to stop himself from slipping off the end of the Unicorn's back and then everything went grey and black and there was nothing at all.

'That,' said the Unicorn in its husky echoing voice, only it was very faint, 'that is absolutely the last time. Never again, *never*!'

It didn't even bother to glance at its own beautiful reflection in the speckled glass, but sank slowly to its knees and then lay on the hard, cold ground of the best coal house with its sides heaving like bellows. Nobody else spoke for a very long while and the silence was only broken by the soft 'tck-tck-tck' of the budgerigars and the distant rumble of the traffic up and down the Earls Court Road.

Sammy sat back against the comforting cold side of the turtles' tank and put his head on his knees while Nell did exactly the same thing with her back to the aviary. It really was very nice to know that one was back on ground level and that there was nothing to fall off at all. It was, in fact, so reassuring that she managed to say, 'Thank you very much for rescuing me, dear Unicorn.'

'Think nothing of it,' the Unicorn replied in a spent voice, 'I could not, after all, leave you to perish. It was my duty to rescue you. The hazards, the dangers, were quite terrible, but naturally I spared no thought for them. Your safety was my only desire.'

'I like that,' said Sammy, raising his head.

'I thought you would,' the Unicorn said, returning to its usual calm manner, and it slowly raised its heavy lids to glance at the mirror.

'And thank you too, Sammy,' said Nell. 'It seemed such a splendid idea to go to Unicorn House and . . . oh . . .'

All three of them now having got their breaths back suddenly thought of the same thing and all three heads turned in the golden gloom of the best coal house to look at the fourth figure, which was lying flat on its face on the chalk marks.

'Oh,' said Nell for the second time.

'Crikey,' said Sammy.

'Dear me,' said the Unicorn, rising gracefully to its hooves, 'Now what?'

Mr Cowgill slowly rolled over onto his back and

laced his fingers behind his head as he gazed dreamily up at the budgerigars which were now flying backwards and forwards and chirruping gently to each other.

'Where am I?' Mr Cowgill said dreamily. 'Are these indeed the Elysian Fields?'

Two pairs of blue eyes and one pair of round white eyes met in the shadows of the best coal house.

'Tell me?' said Mr Cowgill, 'do tell me.'

'Oh crikey, crikey, crikey,' said Sammy.

8. The Kidnappers

'What's the matter with your steak and kidney pudding? Don't you like it? Aren't you feeling well?' asked Uncle Ted.

Sammy mumbled something and went on pushing the meat and suet round his plate.

'Your neck isn't stiff is it?' Uncle Ted demanded.

'No, rather not,' Sammy looked left and right and

tried to pretend that he was eating. Uncle Ted shook his own head and gave himself a second helping.

'There's been a right old do about the blessed Unicorn statue,' he said, 'there's been a whole lot more people round here this morning asking questions, not to mention the telephone going and going. I think it was students myself, some of that long-haired lot that's for ever hanging about the Earls Court Road. Do anything for a lark they would, got no sense of responsibility. Are you sure you're O.K., Sammy? You look very peaky.'

For a moment Sammy was tempted to tell Uncle Ted the whole story, but then he had a sudden horrible vision of what would follow such a disclosure. The police would undoubtedly be brought in and as Sammy himself had in a way 'stolen' the Unicorn—although, he thought bitterly, it was the other way round really, as it was the Unicorn who had started all the trouble—and then one thing would lead to another and Uncle Ted would probably lose his job. Added to which the budgerigars, turtles and fish would undoubtedly be discovered.

'I'm a bit tired,' said Sammy, 'I'll get the sweet. What is it?'

'Yoghurts. Your Aunt says they're good for us, although I can't say I really fancy them myself, so perhaps I won't bother. I'll just slip along and see if the birds are O.K. It's not good for them, you know, being cooped up in the coal house like this.'

'They're—they're fine,' said Sammy. 'I've just been to look at them. Have some cheese.'

'All right. You're a good lad,' said Uncle Ted, a remark which made Sammy feel more guilty than ever. However, this was the least of his worries and all through the washing-up he hardly knew how to contain himself as he was so anxious to get back to the Unicorn and Mr Cowgill to talk matters over. Luckily it was Uncle Ted's half day and when he had said for at least the sixth time, 'Are you sure you don't want to come to the football, Sammy? It's Parsons Green v Fulham North you know . . .'

And Sammy had replied equally firmly, 'No, no thank you honestly, I've promised to see Nell about something.'

Uncle Ted put on his long scarf and collected his rattle and went off and Sammy was free to escape to the coal house. However, being quite a thoughtful boy he did pause to put the rest of the steak and kidney pudding on a plate and to tuck the uneaten yoghurt into his pocket before he left the flat.

He found quite a cosy meeting in progress when he eventually reached the Unicorn's home. The creature was standing with its four legs wide apart, while Nell brushed and combed it. It looked very much more like its old self and was snorting softly as she worked while Mr Cowgill, propped up against the turtles' tank, was just finishing off a bowl of soup.

'Hallo,' he said, licking the spoon, 'that was good, only . . .'

'Have some more,' said Sammy and handed over the steak and kidney.

'Thanks awfully, I'm ravenous,' Mr Cowgill said gratefully. 'It's a funny thing you know but I haven't had much of an appetite for months and months and now for no reason at all I feel starving hungry. It's all part of my being ill I suppose.'

'Um,' said Sammy, glaring at Nell who had begun to giggle, 'now look here, there are a few things we've got to work out . . .'

'Do we have to?' asked Mr Cowgill in a wistful

voice. 'I mean I know all this isn't really happening and I'm just making it up inside my head, but I don't want the dream to end yet, it's so much nicer than real life.'

'But this *is* real,' Sammy said indignantly, 'you haven't made us up. I'm me and she's Nell and the Unicorn's the Unicorn.'

'The *last* Unicorn,' the Unicorn interposed gently, 'which is what, if you'll forgive me mentioning it, makes me rather extra important. I think the left hand side of my mane could do with just a *little* more brushing, dear.'

'O.K.' said Nell and squeezed between Mr Cowgill and the tank and set to work on the silky white hair.

'You see,' said Mr Cowgill, licking up the last scraps of the steak and kidney and accepting the yoghurt, 'that proves it, doesn't it? I mean you can't really expect me to believe that I'm sitting in some kind of shed surrounded by birds and turtles and fish and talking to a Unicorn. I beg your pardon, sir, the *last* Unicorn.'

'Granted,' the Unicorn inclined its head courteously.

'But,' began Sammy and then stopped, because it was quite obvious that Mr Cowgill had firmly made up his mind not to believe the truth and in a way that solved the problem of trying to explain everything to him.

'It's awfully strange,' Mr Cowgill went on, 'but when I was very young I used to enjoy reading about knights and dragons and maidens in distress and all that kind of thing. I had to keep it quiet, of course, or I'd have had the life teased out of me by the other boys at school. They all preferred books about wars and fighting and soldiers blowing each other up. Or at least they *said* they did, but I sometimes wondered . . . Anyway some of my stories had unicorns in them and I always thought they were fascinating creatures . . .'

'Quite right,' the Unicorn agreed, nodding gently.

'And really it was in a way *because* of that feeling that I went to work at the Unicorn Overseas Development Trust Corporation. Of course the firm had nothing to do with heraldry and knighthood and all the rest of it, it was just the name. Does that sound ridiculous?'

'Not at all,' replied Nell, standing back to admire her handiwork, 'that's why I picked Unicorn House out of the telephone book. I thought it might be the place where we could get some help, but it wasn't at all,' and she shivered violently as she remembered the terrifying scene on the roof.

'Now look here,' said Sammy, who felt that it was high time he got a word in, 'first of all that man in the helmet and overalls, the one you called Black . . .'

'That's right, Mr Black, the Chief Security Officer.'

'Well, he was one of Them wasn't he?' Sammy asked the Unicorn.

The creature trembled as violently as Nell had just done and jerked sideways.

'Oh yes,' it said huskily, 'and that was why the moment I landed on the roof of my great temple I was aware of the scent of danger. It was extremely strong. I cannot imagine how I summoned up the courage to return,' and it glanced sideways at Nell who said instantly, 'It was jolly brave.'

'Yes it was,' agreed the Unicorn. 'But for some time now I have sensed that my enemies are closing in about me. Their Magic appears to be growing stronger while mine, alas, is weakening . . .'

A faint chill wind seemed to blow through the small room and even the birds stopped chirping and quarrelling between themselves, while the fish hung motionless in the water and the turtles went still. Sammy felt the hairs on the back of his neck go stiff and in the sudden still silence he could hear Nell's teeth chatter.

'Gone a bit cold in here hasn't it?' said Mr Cowgill, turning up his coat collar and blowing on his hands.

'I couldn't say,' replied the Unicorn, 'I never feel any change in the temperature. I often wonder what it must be like to experience it.' and for some reason it sighed.

'So,' said Sammy, trying to keep a grip on matters, 'so we jolly nearly landed up in an ambush.' A terrible suspicion suddenly crept into his mind as he spoke and he glanced sideways at Mr Cowgill, who now appeared to be nodding off to sleep. As quietly as he could Sammy stepped over the gentleman's highly polished shoes and bent close to the Unicorn and whispered in its pricked ear.

'He,' and he jerked his head towards the figure on the floor, '*he's* not one of Them, is he?'

'No, no,' the Unicorn flicked its ear, 'don't *do* that, it buzzes. No, he's perfectly all right. What you might call a light shade of pale grey really. Something clings to him which is not as it should be, but that could be because he has been close to the man called Black. These things rub off you know. I could never have carried him on my back—oh dear, it still aches quite dreadfully with all your three weights, for I was never meant to transport so many at one go—if he had been my Enemy. I should have shattered into pieces and then we should all have been lost.'

'You can say that again,' agreed Sammy, swallowing

as he remembered the tremendous drop from the top of the skyscraper building, 'but Unicorn, if he's not on Their side, how did he know about the Elysian Fields?'

'I don't know. Why don't you ask him? Only you'd better get a move on, he'll be fast asleep in a tick.'

'Go *on*,' urged Nell, who had been listening to this whispered conversation while she tried to stop her teeth from chattering. It had all been so nice and quiet and comforting while she was grooming the Unicorn, and she had almost forgotten all the terrors of the morning until the temperature of the best coal house had dropped in that frightening way.

Mr Cowgill was obviously extremely tired for Sammy had to shake him quite violently before his head jerked up and he didn't seem to understand the question until it had been repeated three times.

'The Elysian Fields?' he said thickly, 'oh I don't know why I mentioned them. Association of ideas I suppose. Oh,' and he yawned widely. 'Unicorns and Black and White Knights and all the rest of it. I suppose it's all quite logical really. I've been overworking and I'm having a nervous breakdown and so I've gone back to my childhood. Where was I? Oh yes, *my* Elysian Fields would be somewhere sunny and warm and beautiful with mountains in the background and a very blue sea and . . . oooooh . . .' and he yawned again as his head dropped forward onto his knees.

'Oh wake up, do,' Sammy said desperately. 'Where should we start looking?'

'When it all began I suppose, perhaps with William the Conqueror and *his* Knights, as they were the first in the field so to speak in this country. He built the Tower of London you know. I say, do you think I could just have a short nap? I can't keep my eyes open . . .'

It was perfectly true, for even as he spoke Mr Cowgill's eyes rolled in a most alarming manner and in spite of Sammy's efforts his head thudded down against his knees.

'You won't get much more out of him,' the Unicorn said knowledgeably, 'I've seen Knights behave in exactly the same manner after a battle or a tournament. Full of get up and go one moment and out on their feet the next. Sometimes they slept for days just where they had fallen and their armour got terribly rusty with the dew. The only answer is to leave them be. To be truthful I feel a bit the same myself. Pardon me,' and it too yawned hugely with the result that Nell and Sammy found their jaws aching for there is nothing more catching than a yawn.

'But we can't leave him *here*,' Sammy said.

Keeping the Unicorn, the birds, fish and turtles hidden was enough of a worry, let alone hiding a respectable gentleman from the City.

'Then why not put him outside?' suggested the Unicorn and shut its beautiful eyes.

Sammy and Nell looked at each other. When all was said and done it had been a very long exhausting and frightening day and they too needed a bit of time in which to recover from all that had happened. All the same Mr Cowgill had come to their rescue twice, and it hardly seemed fair to just dump him somewhere, even if they knew where to do it.

'We could put him in the Gardens, I suppose,' Sammy said doubtfully.

'Supposing it rained? He'd catch his death of cold. He's not like the Unicorn,' Nell replied.

'Then where . . .'

They stared at each other in the gathering gloom until Sammy said slowly.

'There's an empty flat on the top floor next to your grandmother's. The people have gone abroad for a couple of months or something. But supposing someone found out . . .'

By someone he meant Uncle Ted who, without being in the least aware of it, was already in trouble up to his ears.

'He saved my life,' said Nell, 'and yours and the Unicorn's too.'

'Drat the Unicorn!'

'Hush, it'll hear you!'

'I don't care. Oh very well. I'll get the key, oh dear, oh dear . . .'

It was no easy matter to urge the exhausted Mr Cowgill to his feet or to direct his dragging footsteps to the lift and Sammy felt his muscles twitch as he heard the roar of the rush hour traffic grow in volume down the Earls Court Road as somehow he and Nell managed to push and shove and pull their unwelcome guest into the small iron cage. And the lift seemed slower and more wheezy than ever as it climbed up the centre of Leo Mansions with its nasty habit of pausing between floors as it did so.

'Now I know how a burglar feels,' Sammy whispered.

'Or a kidnapper,' replied Nell, who was on the very edge of bursting into nervous giggles as she tried to hold Mr Cowgill upright. He would keep shifting first to one side and then the other.

'I never heard of two children kidnapping a grown up person,' said Sammy. 'Oh crikey, we're there . . .'

The top landing appeared to be deserted and somehow, with a great deal of heavy breathing, he and Nell managed to get Mr Cowgill into the empty flat which smelt dusty and warm, but somehow unlived in at the same time.

'I know just what the Unicorn meant,' Sammy said breathlessly, 'when it said it wasn't strong enough to carry three people. One, two, three and onto that sofa . . .'

Mr Cowgill fell quite heavily, but he didn't appear to mind and after Sammy had lifted his feet up after him and Nell had thoughtfully found a rug and tucked it round him he only stirred slightly and said, 'How very, very kind. Goodnight.'

'Now what?' said Sammy as he and Nell, both rather pale and very shaky, shut the door of the no longer empty flat, after leaving the key on the hall table.

'Nothing,' Nell replied firmly. 'No more adventures, no more looking for Elysian Fields and all the rest of it. I vote we have a rest for a bit.'

'Agreed.'

They shook hands solemnly and Nell went into her own flat while Sammy, as the lift had vanished back to the ground floor and he wasn't supposed to use it anyway, ran down the stairs, round and round until he reached the basement.

Luckily they were both unaware of two quite different developments which might have disturbed them considerably.

The first was that a certain door on the top landing had not been entirely closed and that a pair of bright eyes had witnessed the hiding away of Mr Cowgill, and the second was that the newspaper sellers in the Earls Court Road had already got on display some notices which read.

CITY TYCOON VANISHES

SURPRISE DEVELOPMENTS IN U.O.D.T. . . .

9. *The Enemy comes closer*

For the next few days a great calm descended over Leo Mansions as far as Sammy and Nell were concerned. As neither of them read the newspapers they were quite unaware that a great rumpus had broken out in the City of London about the affairs of the Unicorn Overseas Development Trust and that hundreds of thousands of pounds were changing hands and that a great many people all over the world were being shifted about in their jobs. There were only two things about which they were either certain of or at all interested in and they were that first, the Unicorn appeared to have gone into a kind of trance and neither spoke nor moved when addressed.

'Gone back to being a statue again and just as well too . . .' said Sammy.

And secondly that there was no sound at all from the flat where they had hidden Mr Cowgill.

'I've listened outside the front door every morning,' reported Nell, 'and all you can hear, and you have to listen ever so carefully, is him snoring. How long *can* people sleep for?'

'I don't know and I don't care,' replied Sammy, 'let's do something nice and ordinary . . . Magic's too exhausting if you ask me. Where shall we go today?'

There are a great many things you can do in London, and without spending any money at all if you put your mind to it. So they fed the ducks in Green Park and the swans in Battersea Park and watched the Changing of the Guard outside Buckingham Palace—although this made Nell feel a bit sad as all the horses were so beautiful with their gleaming coats and she did so long for a pony of her own—with the result that Sammy had to walk her away very fast to the Science Museum where he could look at all the models of steam engines.

Every now and again they made a faint-hearted attempt to track down the Elysian Fields, but as Sammy so rightly pointed out, there was no trace of them in any of the reference books they consulted so how could they be expected to find them?

'But we ought to do *something*,' argued Nell, who had now quite recovered from her fright on top of the Unicorn House, 'we can't just let it go back to being a statue again. I say, Sammy, you can see right across the Thames from here . . .'

Which was hardly surprising as they were on top of the Monument from where you can get the most magnificent view all over London.

'I don't see why we should at all,' Sammy replied grumpily and turned to look eastwards, which was a bad mistake as there, looking grey and magnificent, was the Tower of London.

'But don't you think we should?' Nell asked timidly after a very long pause during which a number of pigeons had fluttered down onto the parapet, making soft cooing noises and stretching their green and purple necks. 'I mean it does expect us to help and it did rescue us.'

'Um, um, um,' replied Sammy who was in that very sorely tried state of mind when half of him knew that he ought to do something while the other half hung back. Adventures are all very well when they happen to other people, but they're quite a different cup of tea when they happen to you and when you have been through two very nasty experiences you start to get cautious. But all the same, duty is duty and it's not every day that a Unicorn—the last Unicorn at that—appeals to you for help.

'Oh very *well*,' Sammy said furiously, 'only don't blame me if everything goes wrong, that's all. Come on, race you down.'

As some of the interest in the vanishing statue appeared to have died down, and the Police were no longer paying daily visits to the flats, Uncle Ted was starting to get restive about his livestock and that evening he said to a somewhat abstracted Sammy, 'I think we could bring the birds and all the rest of them back in here, don't you?'

'What?' said Sammy, blinking. Uncle Ted repeated his question and then to Sammy's horror, added, 'I know you've been looking after them, lad, but it can't be good for 'em stuck away out there. Let's bring 'em back tonight, eh?'

Sammy's eyes bulged, but no sound would come out of his mouth at all except a kind of strangled 'Wh-wha-what?' and it was Aunt Jessie who unwittingly saved the situation by saying, 'Oh leave the boy alone, Ted, he looks fagged to death. There, there Sammy don't you fret lad, you'll get a letter from your father in the next day or two. I know it's not like him not to write every week, but you can't trust these foreign post offices.'

'Well, we'll move 'em tomorrow eh?' said Uncle Ted, 'now what do you fancy for the Pools this week, eh?'

'So we've got to do something,' Sammy said the following morning when he arrived on Nell's doorstep, 'and the first thing is to move the birds and all the rest of them . . .'

The birds, fish and turtles objected to having their homes transported in their usual manner and were just as heavy to carry but throughout the very exhausting operation the Unicorn stayed entirely motionless. In fact it really did look as if it had been transformed back into a statue until Nell said fiercely into its ear.

'Come on, wake up for goodness sake.'

The ear twitched and the Unicorn stirred, shivered and slowly moved its beautiful head.

'I have been dreaming,' it said huskily, 'of sylvan glades, green grass and stilly pools wherein I saw my own reflection instead of which you recall me to this,' and it glared quite crossly at the speckled mirror, the antlers, the baby's chair and the cardboard boxes, adding, 'It's not at all what I am accustomed to, not at all . . .'

'That's what I call gratitude,' said Sammy, 'we do our best to save it, to rescue it and all that, but it doesn't really care at all.'

'It does,' Nell replied, 'at least it cares about something because it's not like it was you know. It's going quite grey round its forelocks, poor thing. Oh Sammy are you sure this'll work?'

'I'm not sure about anything at all,' Sammy snapped, 'but it's the only lead we've got. Mr Cowgill said to start with the Tower of London because that's when all the knighthood business began so maybe we will find the Elysian Fields there. Gosh, I do hope so.'

For like the Unicorn, and in spite of several days' rest from magic, Sammy felt rather out of sorts. Not ill exactly, but jumpy and nervous and a bit frightened as if something unpleasant was going to happen, and he couldn't shake out of his mind the way in which the creature had said its powers were weakening and that the Enemy were slowly, stealthily closing in round them. If only they knew who the Enemy were it would be something, but the only one they had so far been able to identify was Mr Black and he was miles away in the City of London and couldn't possibly know that the creature he was out to capture had gained at least some kind of sanctuary in Earls Court. Sammy had another worry too, a very private one which somehow he couldn't share with anybody, not even Uncle Ted. And that was that he hadn't had a letter from his Dad for seventeen days which was extremely odd as he usually got one every week.

'Oh come on do,' Sammy snapped, getting up and going over to the Unicorn and giving it quite a hard push so that it snorted and rolled its eyes reproachfully.

'Gosh, you're crabby,' said Nell. 'What *is* the matter?'

Sammy thought of telling her the truth and then in the same second decided against it. She was only a child and she'd probably get in a real old stew if she realised just how nasty things could be should they find themselves surrounded by the Enemy forces, and his father was his own business; so instead he said the second thing which came into his head which was, 'Well, Mr Cowgill. People can't last for long without food you know, and supposing he really *is* ill? I expect people still snore even if they are unwell.'

'I'll go up and have a look at him,' volunteered Nell.

'You can't. He's got the key inside the flat! And anyway . . .'

'Then I'll look through the letter box. You stay here, I won't be a tick.'

In fact Nell was only too glad to do something nice and ordinary like checking on Mr Cowgill as it meant putting off the moment when they would once again be landed in the middle of some magic, which, as she knew from past experience, was certain to be far too exciting for her tastes. So Nell went running up to the ground floor and as for once the lift happened to be waiting there she got into it and pressed the top button. It wheezed and shook and rose so slowly and stuck for such a long time between the fourth and fifth floors that Nell's small finger was poised over the Alarm Button and then with a final groan it continued on its journey to the top. There was nobody about and the only sound—apart from the thudding of the traffic—was the noise of rifles banging which meant that Nell's grandmother had settled down in front of the television set to watch her favourite Cowboy series, so Nell closed the lift gates as gently as possible and tip-toed over to the front door of the 'empty' flat and lifted the letter box.

It really was astonishingly quiet in there and Nell, holding her breath, was just starting to wonder if Mr Cowgill really had become ill and so stopped snoring, when she heard very faintly a 'snort-snort' and at the same time something very softly tapped her on the shoulder.

Poor Nell spun round, her heart thundering and all the colour going out of her cheeks.

'I wonder,' said a low voice, 'if I could speak with you a moment? There is somebody here who would like to speak with you. Yes?'

'I, I, I. Oh, oh, oh,' said Nell.

'Please?' and a hand was laid delicately on Nell's arm and she was drawn gently, but firmly into the flat next door to the one where Mr Cowgill lay deep in sleep, so deep indeed that like the Unicorn he might have been turned into a statue. The front door clicked shut and then there was no sound at all except for the traffic and the voice on Mrs Bates' television which was saying, 'Hands up, I've got you cornered . . .'

Downstairs in the best coal house Sammy waited and waited and waited while the evening shadows stole softly across the sky and the small area in Unicorn Gardens, which was where the Unicorn had once stood and was now enclosed by a wooden fence, vanished into the darkness. Up and down the Earls Court Road the shops put up their 'Closed' notices and the number of people getting out of the underground station grew and grew until the pavements were as crowded as the road. At Boofers Self Service Aunt Jess rang up her till and thankfully watched the last of the shoppers leave and at the other end of the Road Uncle Ted, who had been putting in new nylon sash cords in Block 7 Leo Mansions, decided that he'd do just one more landing and then that would be his lot for the day.

And in the coal house the Unicorn lifted its handsome head and turned round a couple of times and whinnied softly in much the same way as it had done in the lion's cage at the Zoo.

'What is it?' asked Sammy, who had been cracking his fingers, a trick much admired by the other boys at school, but deplored by Aunty Jess.

'Danger,' said the Unicorn in a very quiet, husky whisper, 'Danger. It is coming closer. I can feel it, I can feel it . . .' And it suddenly reared up on its hind legs in such an alarming way that Sammy had to dodge quickly to get out of the way of its delicate hooves.

'Nell?' demanded Sammy. 'Is it Nell?'

'I don't know, I don't know . . .' the creature's eyes rolled right back in its head, 'I think not. But it grows closer. Quick, quick Sammy, go and look . . .'

Sammy went like an arrow from its bow. Once again he was aware that a terrible coldness had stolen into the air and by the time he reached the ground floor of the flats his teeth were jiggling together like ice cubes being shaken in a bowl. Even as he reached the shadowy hall the main doors were pushed open so violently that they crashed back against the walls and some instinct made Sammy freeze into position. A man marched across the stone floor, the sound of his steel-edged shoes echoing and in spite of the half-light Sammy was able to see the man's face fairly distinctly. This time he was wearing a motor cyclist's crash helmet and overall, but he was unmistakable, and without pausing to think Sammy turned and ran, his own plimsolled feet luckily making no sound at all.

'What is it? Have they come?' demanded the Unicorn, flecks of sweat on its white head. 'Is it my Enemy? Tell me!'

'Yes,' Sammy panted, 'He's here. Mr Black . . .'

'Ahh,' the Unicorn drew in a long trembling breath, 'I knew it was about to happen. They've captured me and this is the end, the end of the last Unicorn. Here—in this place,' and it jerked back its head and snorted so violently that the speckled mirror misted over and its reflection became blurred.

'Not yet they haven't', Sammy replied, 'although I don't know how he discovered that you . . . but that doesn't matter now. We've got to get away . . .' And he plumped down on his knees and picked up the very end of the bit of chalk and wrote the first thing that came into his head while the Unicorn wheeled about him.

TOWER OF LONDON.

As both Sammy and the Unicorn were quite panicky by this time Sammy nearly slid clean over the creature's back, but somehow he managed to grasp its mane with his shaking hands and within no time at all the best coal house was spinning round and round and vanishing into darkness.

Neither of them heard above their heads an impatient 'bzz-bzz' as a gauntletted finger pushed the lift button for the third time.

10. The Prisoners in the Tower

The Unicorn was perfectly correct in saying that its magic was on the wane for instead of the usual swift, if rather sea-sick, transportation from one place to another, Sammy discovered to his dismay that when he opened his eyes he was not, as he had fondly believed, safe and sound inside the Tower of London, but flying in a somewhat zig-zag manner over the skyscrapers, turrets, church spires and very ordinary roofs of the City. Luckily it was almost night time and as nobody ever, or very rarely, looks upwards at the sky, their erratic progress was unnoticed by the rush hour workers far below.

'Oh crikey,' said Sammy and tightened his grip. He also realised for the first time what it must have been like for Nell to be poised on the roof of the Unicorn Building. 'Oh crikey,' he repeated and closed his eyes again.

'I can't help it,' said the Unicorn, glancing over its shining white shoulder, 'I told you my magic was growing weaker. Oh dear . . .' it added uncertainly.

'Oh dear *what*?'

'Nothing,' replied the Unicorn untruthfully and concentrated on its downward path. It managed a four-point, very accurate landing, however, and then shook itself delicately to show that journey's end had been reached. Sammy slid down and leant against the creature's flanks and the pair of them took several deep breaths before they said anything more. The Unicorn had come to earth on the soft springy turf outside the low, right-angled house where Queen Anne Boleyn had once been kept more or less a prisoner. The only other living things in sight were three very large, black ravens and a Yeoman warder who was just going off duty, whistling softly between his teeth. He went on his way and vanished into the shadows and then there was a soft clink-clank and Sammy whispered, 'What's that?'

'Shh . . .' said the Unicorn. 'Hold fast, desist, in other words shut up. Sorry, I learnt that from the starlings in my Gardens. Their grasp of slang is wide, but not very polite I'm afraid. Anyway it was only a gate being locked up for the night.'

The ravens who had watched this unexpected arrival in some astonishment now began to walk up and down, opening their clipped wings and making loud 'caw-caw' noises.

'You shut up too,' snorted the Unicorn and the big black carrions blinked and then did as they were told although they ruffled up their ebony feathers and looked angry.

'Are we safe?' Sammy asked at last. There was quite a cold wind blowing in off the river and bending the turf, but strangely enough he hardly felt it.

'Quite safe. In a way,' the Unicorn said reluctantly, 'although there is one small point I feel I should mention,' and it coughed delicately, 'although I don't quite know *how* to mention it . . . perhaps I could put it in this manner . . .'

'Don't bother,' said Sammy letting out a great gasp of relief. 'Now look here, Unicorn, we were jolly nearly captured this time, so please, please get a move on and find out if your Elysian Fields are round here. It certainly *looks* a very safe place.'

'Yes but . . .' said the Unicorn, flicking back a lock of white mane, 'I do feel that I *should* tell you . . .'

'Just get on,' ordered Sammy, so the Unicorn shut its mouth and trotted over to the ravens while Sammy got his bearings and then stretched up his arms. He felt quite different from usual. It was almost as though he had become very light on his feet and as he had always been rather heavy this made a nice change. Added to which he couldn't for the life of him remember why he'd been in such a panic to escape from all that old Black Magic lot. Really there'd been a lot of fuss about nothing and as this was the first time he'd ever been to the Tower of London he might as well make the most of it after all!

So Sammy floated away, there was no other way of describing his progress, to explore the battlements, and he very quickly discovered he didn't even have to bother about climbing the stairs as a simple little push with one foot sent him soaring upwards. He looked over the parapet at the river Thames and all the twinkling lights on the roads which were the home-bound traffic and then decided that he would like to examine the crown jewels. He knew, of course, that they were extremely closely guarded by electric eyes and all sorts of burglar alarms, but all the same no sooner had he thought that he would care to examine them than, bob-bob-bob—and his feet appeared to know the way perfectly well—and he was inside that great treasure chest.

And it really was something to see too. Diamonds flashed like spot lights, their multi-coloured reflections shimmering on the ceiling above his head, while the great gold and silver plates, goblets and chalices gleamed before his eyes.

Sammy Jenkins of Earls Court gazed at the Crown of England, at the precious stone which the Black Prince had once worn in battle and at the mace and the orb that are carried at a Monarch's coronation. There was nobody to hinder his view, no tourists, no Yeoman warder to move him on. He could look and look as much as he wanted and it was as if the past, the present and the future were all mixed up together.

'Crikey,' said Sammy, 'golly, I say . . .'

He walked round and round staring at all the fabulous treasures which have been accumulated over the centuries and every one of which has a fascinating—and quite often blood-stained—past, and it was as if all the dull old history that he'd reluctantly absorbed at school had come to life.

And while Sammy was staring a chill wind came whipping up the river and set all the tugs, barges and ships rocking and nodding as they lay at anchor. It made a whistling sound through the great cranes which were at rest in the Pool of London and it crept inside the warehouses and sent the rats and mice scuttling. It whined over the rooftops and under the eaves and it moaned and it groaned round the statues and carvings of both the old buildings and the new. It sighed over the lions in Trafalgar Square and it disturbed the quiet water of St. James' Park and the still surfaces of the Serpentine and Battersea Park lake, and the animals in the Zoo at Regents Park huddled together and the lions in particular paced up and down. Even the budgerigars and canaries, parrots and mina birds in private houses ruffled up their feathers, while the cats' furs stood up on end and dogs growled and grew restless. It was as though a great unease settled over all the sprawling miles of London from Charing Cross to Ponders End, from Piccadilly Circus to Ealing North.

'Funny sort of weather,' the home-bound commuters said to each other, 'well, it's probably the time of year . . .'

The Unicorn felt it most of all and it pranced up and down on its delicate hooves and tossed its mane, because it sensed what was happening.

'They're coming,' it said to the ravens, 'my enemies —you're black in feather, but not in heart and *you* know . . .'

The oldest raven cocked its head and looked up knowingly as it croaked hoarsely, reminiscing about the past. It was so rarely that it got an opportunity to talk to another truly knowledgeable creature.

'Ha,' the Unicorn replied, tossing back its mane, '*You* can't remember. You're no age at all. *You* never knew that poor young lady, Mistress Anne Boleyn, being taken to the block—and not so far from where you're standing now either—but I did. And the one who came after her, and only a child *she* was, Catherine Howard and then there was the Lady Jane Grey . . . off with their heads, off with their heads . . . that was all the cry in those days. And I can go a long way further back than that. Oh, I could tell a tale or two about the Princes in the Tower—why *they* weren't murdered. It was no such thing, but we Unicorns weren't supposed to have eyes in our heads, or ears with which to listen or tongues with which to tell. That's why they got rid of us I daresay and turned the lions back into poor dumb creatures, not that *that* took a lot of doing as they were downright stupid to begin with. So now there is only me left and no Elysian Fields in which to find sanctuary after all . . .'

'Caw,' the oldest raven replied sadly lifting its wings.

'Yes, I daresay,' the Unicorn pivoted on its small hooves, 'you may well want to get rid of me. I'm only an embarrassment. YOU've turned respectable haven't you? Showing off to the tourists and getting your weekly ration of food from the Ministry of Works. The carrion crows told me all about *you*, they call you their Civil Servant cousins!'

At this jeering remark which the Unicorn, quite forgetting to be careful, delivered in a full pitched husky tone, the three ravens took immediate offence and began to run round in circles, their wings heaving.

'Go on, go on,' the Unicorn responded, becoming in its turn equally put out, 'it's O.K. for you to get so hoity-toity, but just wait till you get turned into marble and have to spend hundreds of years pretending to be a statue with everybody making remarks about you! Why, I can recall when this fortress of yours was being built and we creatures were respected and magic was magic and knights at arms . . . oh crikey!'

By this time not only the Unicorn, but the ravens too had become quite carried away and all four of them were talking at the tops of their voices and making a great deal more noise than was usual within the Tower of London, with the inevitable result that a patch of golden light suddenly erupted across the grass and a voice shouted, 'Who goes there? Yeoman warders to arms!'

And a great many not-so-young but still extremely fit men appeared, fairly tumbling over themselves as they gripped their pikestaffs to go into action.

'Oh lawks,' said the Unicorn and dipped its head towards the oldest raven, which hesitated for a second, then whispered hoarsely before hopping away to join its two companions who were vainly trying to escape from the bright and quite blinding lights.

Sammy, who had all this time been gazing entranced at the fabulous treasures in the jewel house, heard the commotion and jerked to attention. It only took three bounds for him to rejoin the Unicorn, which was now prancing and circling up on the battlements with its mane flowing in the strong wind off the river.

'What's going on?' demanded Sammy. 'Have you found . . .?'

'Found out a bit,' replied the Unicorn, 'not much, but a bit. They may have black feathers, but their hearts are white. It's no good hanging about though.'

'Are your Elysian Fields here?'

'In a manner of speaking. They existed in this place once upon a time, but it was a long while ago and there's been far too much bloodshed since then. There's no tranquillity here now, that's certain. No sylvan glades, no . . . I say, what was that?'

'Some kind of searchlight, I think. Who are all those people shouting?'

Sammy leaned over the parapet and then blinked as a very strong light shone directly in his eyes.

'Guards, this place always *was* full of them. Guards to keep people in, guards to keep people out. Guards to take people captive.'

'And now they're after us,' Sammy said, staring down at the courtyard below which was swarming with not only Yeoman warders but with security officers as well.

'I don't think we have any cause to worry,' said the Unicorn, 'as I was trying to explain to you earlier . . .'

'Come on,' Sammy commanded, 'and quick . . .'

'Yes, but . . .' the Unicorn began, 'as I was trying . . .'

Sammy made a grab for the creature's tail, but to his surprise it seemed to slide through his fingers. He lunged again, but even as he did so the leading warder reached the parapet not two feet away, and then as Sammy retreated towards the stonework the man, instead of reaching forwards and taking him prisoner, leapt away with his eyes becoming as round as the Unicorn's. He staggered slightly and his pike slipped through his fingers and his face became as white as his ruff in the pale moonlight.

'Oh, oh, oh,' said the Yeoman warder and put his hands over his face.

Sammy bent down and picked up the staff to return it to him but at the same moment the Unicorn sidled into position alongside the astonished Sammy and said fiercely, 'Get up, get up or at least try to.'

'But, but why didn't he take me prisoner?' asked Sammy, gaping at the warder who was now retreating step by step away from the pair of them.

'I did try to tell you—there, you're light as a feather and what a relief *that* is—but you wouldn't listen. Hold tight, if you can. Ready?'

'Ready,' agreed Sammy, although he was somewhat impeded by the pikestaff.

'Good. Then hold your hand up to the moon.'

Sammy did as he was told and then his eyes goggled even more than the Yeoman warder's had done, for clean through his own somewhat grubby palm he could see the thin silver crescent in the sky.

'I did try,' the Unicorn said, bracing itself and then jumping stiff legged into the night, 'I did *try* and explain but you just wouldn't listen. It's all your fault really. Not all of you is here. It's just one of those things you know . . .'

Sammy gulped and held up his transparent hand against the hurrying clouds. It was just as the Unicorn had said, only part of him was visible . . .

Nell, who had been dozing in the coal house, jerked herself awake and saw the familiar dark whirling cloud of the Unicorn start to take on shape before the speckled mirror.

'And about time too,' she said, 'I've been waiting ages and ages. Oh!'

'Don't be upset,' the Unicorn said, settling down into its white marble self, 'We've been on a journey and . . .'

'I can see you have,' Nell agreed, 'you look awful, I mean . . .' she amended hastily, 'a bit tired. But what's happened to Sammy? He's not all here.'

'I know,' Sammy said crossly, 'there's no need to

rub it in. Something went wrong. Am I still . . .?' and he held out both arms as he slid off the Unicorn's cold back.

'You're not quite all of you,' Nell said in a trembling voice. 'I can see the reindeer's horns through your head. Oh Sammy, what have you done?'

'It's not me, it's it. Its magic's gone wrong. We've been to the Tower of London and it wasn't any use at all, in fact we nearly got captured. And anyway where've *you* been?'

'I've been busy,' said Nell in a rather guilty voice. 'I've been down the Portobello Market actually and I've met . . . but that doesn't matter now. Oh Sammy, are you going to be half invisible for ever and ever?'

'Ask it.'

'*I* can't tell,' the Unicorn replied, 'He wouldn't listen. I tried to explain, I really did. And the raven said . . .'

'Never mind the raven,' said the half invisible Sammy staring at his own feet through which he could see the chalk marks on the floor, 'what about *me*? Uncle Ted and Aunt Jess really will go mad if they see me like this. It's all your fault! You get me out of it. Go on. Hurry up. Make me visible again.'

There was a long long pause during which Nell and the shadowy see-through Sammy stared at the Unicorn so hard that its ears and its tail, now rather grey round the edges, flicked backwards and forwards.

'I can't,' the Unicorn said at last in a very low husky voice. 'I told you before that my Enemies were closing in and that they've taken a great deal of my magic away from me. I can't do anything. If the worst comes to the worst,' and the creature swallowed deeply, 'Sammy may have to stay half invisible for the rest of his life. I'm terribly sorry . . .'

'Oh glory,' said Sammy and sank slowly to the floor where Nell could see the chalk marks quite clearly through his feet, 'oh glory. Now what?'

A long silence descended over the best coal house.

11. *See-Through Sammy*

Sammy was so worried about this new predicament that he completely forgot about the earlier arrival of Mr Black. Discovering that one has been transformed into a ghost is enough to drive everything else out of one's thoughts and the Unicorn, on its part, was too exhausted and dispirited to want to do anything but go to sleep. It had, in fact, almost reached the stage of just not caring what happened to it. While Nell, of course, knew nothing of Mr Black's arrival at the flats. She had a great deal to tell Sammy, but this was quite obviously not the time to do it, so she put the pikestaff neatly to one side and tried to think of a solution.

'*I* know,' she said slowly, 'I'll tell your uncle and aunt that you're having supper with Granny and me and we've asked you to spend the night in our flat.'

'Your grandmother'd have a dozen fits if she saw me like this!'

'But she won't silly. She won't see you at all, because we'll only be pretending. You can spend the night here. Or,' and Nell clapped her hands, 'up in the empty top flat, Number 24. Mr Cowgill'll never know because he's still sleeping. Oh, we can't get in.'

'That's no problem,' Sammy said with a faint smile, 'watch . . .'

And he got up and walked straight through the wall and into the coal house next door and then re-appeared while Nell was still staring at the brickwork.

'But,' Sammy went on, feeling slightly cheered by Nell's dumbfounded expression, 'but Uncle Ted'll think it's barmy. I mean why *should* I spend the night on the top floor when it's only six flights down to my own bed?'

'If,' said the Unicorn in a weary voice, 'if it's any consolation, now that you are only half here so to speak, then you will probably discover that your loving relations only care about you half as much as they did. Magic may go wrong, but it often makes up for it in other ways. White magic that is, not the other kind,' and it shivered slightly and then closed its eyes, its nose dropping so that its long horn came to rest on the speckled mirror with a squeaking sound.

'Well I like that,' Sammy said indignantly, meaning that he didn't like it at all, 'and I bet it's not true. Well, let's try then . . .'

But it was *perfectly* true for when five minutes later a somewhat flushed Nell knocked on the front door of the basement flat and with her fingers crossed behind her back asked for permission for Sammy to spend the night on the top floor, all Uncle Ted said was, 'We were starting to wonder where he'd got to. It's not like Sammy to miss his supper, although he's not the only one by a long chalk. My birds, you know . . .' and he laid his finger against the side of his nose and winked. Nell winked back. 'And all the others, they're right off their food this evening. Not a chirp or a sound from the lot of them. I can't make it out. I daresay being stuck out in the coal house didn't suit 'em. It's very strange. Aunt Jess and I are worried, very worried as to what's got into them. Here, hold on, you'd better have the lad's pyjamas and toothbrush and that. Very worried we are!'

'But not about me. Oh no,' said Sammy in a very injured tone of voice when Nell reported back with his night things. '*I* see.'

Nell very wisely didn't reply and Sammy, with a last indignant 'Hm! See you in the morning then . . .' went bounding up the stairs like a balloon. Half invisible or not he still had a very real appetite and as he passed through the front door and into the top flat he suddenly remembered that he should have asked Nell if she could spare some supper. He looked round for Mr Cowgill, but there was no sign of him at all apart from some rather squashed cushions on the sofa where, presumably, he had enjoyed his days and nights of sleep.

'Hm,' said Sammy again, 'now where's *he* gone? Probably the Unicorn's old magic has made him vanish completely. Oh . . .' and then Sammy suddenly remembered the earlier arrival of Mr Black and he felt his half visible blood run cold, and even as he did so he heard Nell knocking on the front door across the landing and her Grandmother's voice saying, 'There you are, dear. Your father rang up only half an hour ago—I wish you'd been here. Did you have a lovely time in the Portobello Market? It *was* kind of them to ask you. Come and tell me all about it,' and the door was shut, so it was too late to have a further word with Nell.

'Oh dear, oh dear, oh dear,' said Sammy and walked clean through the wall to the kitchen in his agitation. However, his nose, ghost-like or not, was still perfectly capable of sniffing a quite delicious smell and it led him to the stove where a large casserole was bubbling softly to itself. Sammy looked at it, shut the oven door, walked backwards through the refrigerator and out through the television set and had a short talk with himself.

'It wouldn't *really* be stealing,' said the half invisible Sammy to his wispy reflection in a mirror. 'I could pay him back sometime.' By him, he meant Mr Cowgill. 'And anyway he couldn't eat it all and I *am* jolly hungry . . .' And he rubbed his see-through stomach with a ghostly hand. 'Perhaps he wouldn't mind all *that* much . . .'

It was a perfectly delicious meal, although unlike anything that Sammy had ever eaten before as it was full of spices which even Boofers Super Market didn't sell. And after he had eaten a scrupulously fair half share Sammy was too sleepy to feel worried or frightened about anything more so he passed a flannel over his face and cleaned his teeth (which wasn't all that easy to do as he kept putting the brush right through them until he realised that the only method was to do the whole thing with his eyes shut) and then he took off his clothes and got into his pyjamas and took the dust sheet off the bed and climbed between the blankets and within a matter of seconds was fast asleep.

It was dawn, a pale grey chilly dawn that crept reluctantly over the roof tops of London, when Sammy woke up. He felt rather odd, as though he had grown heavier during the night, and for a moment or two he couldn't think where he was and then he became aware of a voice saying, 'Hallo, what are you doing here?'

And there at his side was Mr Cowgill. At least what appeared to be Mr Cowgill, for he was quite different from the pale, frowning man that Sammy remembered. The lines round his eyes had gone and there was colour in his cheeks and he looked a great deal younger than he had done before.

'Sleeping,' said Sammy.

'Oh yes, I can see that. I wondered who'd eaten half my evening meal. Wasn't it delicious? Did you ever eat food like it? It's all *her* doing. She's a smashing cook.'

'Who is *her*?' asked Sammy struggling upright.

'My Princess,' Mr Cowgill said simply. 'At last, after all these years I've found her. You look a bit strange, old chap. Are you all right?'

Sammy held up a hand hopefully, but he could still see Mr Cowgill's now healthy face through it although not very clearly, so he braced himself and said.

'I'm half invisible. Sorry.'

'Think nothing of it,' Mr Cowgill replied. 'It's all

part of my nervous breakdown I expect. Just as the Unicorn and my Princess are, but I don't want to wake up properly just yet. Would you like some breakfast?'

'Rather. But,' and Sammy slid his legs out of bed, 'but you know you have been sleeping an awful lot. We've listened to you through the letter box and you've snored and snored. Don't you feel better now?'

'Oh yes, immeasurably,' replied Mr Cowgill from the kitchen, 'One egg or two? She brings them into me, you know, my Princess. She's been feeding me all the time.'

'Well, I'm glad about that,' said Sammy, pulling on his jeans, 'we were afraid you might die of hunger.'

'Oh no, quite the opposite I assure you. Why, I haven't eaten so well for years and years. I was always so wrought up and tired, but not any more. Three rashers of bacon each I think . . .'

As Mr Cowgill didn't seem to be in the least upset at having breakfast with a half invisible boy it was a very contented meal and at the finish Mr Cowgill pushed aside his cup and said, 'I really cannot thank you enough, all of you, for what you have done for me. Naturally, I realise that one day I shall have to return to the real world, although I cannot and will not go back to the City, but I now see my way perfectly clearly. I shall go to the Isles of Greece which I have always wanted to visit, and I shall paint. I have some money put aside and it will be quite sufficient for me to live on although to make everything really Elysian I should have my Princess with me.'

'What's her name?' Sammy asked politely, as he scooped up the last of the honey onto his toast.

'I've never enquired. She suddenly appeared at my side with a bowl of soup and from that moment on...'

Mr Cowgill sighed and smiled, 'I knew that at last I had found her. She is so gentle, so quiet . . . but that's enough of that. What are your ambitions?'

'To find the Elysian Fields so that the Unicorn can gain sanctuary and to become all me again,' replied Sammy, putting his hand up against the sugar bowl. Was it his imagination or did he look a bit more solid than before?'

'Yes, I do see that it must be awkward to be only, if you'll forgive me saying so, only *half* there. You were quite whole the last time we met, I remember. Is there anything at all that I can do to help?'

'I wish there was,' Sammy replied glumly. 'It's quite fun in a way, but it's jolly awkward too. I don't see how I can go back to school and I'm sure my father won't like it when he comes home. I can walk straight through walls you know.'

'You *can't*!' said Mr Cowgill admiringly. 'That was always something I wanted to do when I was your age. Do let me see!'

'O.K.' said Sammy, feeling not only very full of breakfast, but also rather proud of himself as it's not everybody who can vanish through solid bricks and mortar. 'Watch this . . . ouch.'

He started off in a rather showing-off manner, but his bouncy footsteps of the previous evening were no longer quite so light and his encounter with the wall made him feel rather breathless. So he stood still for a moment and then gathered himself together and launched himself again at the pale green stripes of the sitting-room and although he felt distinct resistance, rather like trying to pass through a jelly, Sammy did indeed manage to vanish.

'Bravo,' said Mr Cowgill enthusiastically. 'Bravo. Excellent. Do it again. Quite astonishing. Of course it's only part of my dream, but it is great fun. Come on Sammy, once more!'

But no boy reappeared through the wallpaper and for no apparent reason Mr Cowgill felt a distinct cold shiver run down his backbone. Deep down inside himself he was perfectly certain that everything that had happened during the last days—or was it weeks—was really only happening in his imagination. After all, being rescued by a Unicorn and a *talking* Unicorn at that, and meeting two very nice young people in some kind of coal shed, not to mention being fed by a beautiful Princess, could only happen in dreams. And yet, at the very same moment that all this was going through his mind, Mr Cowgill suddenly realised that the sunlight which was falling on his hand was warm and that the coffee cup before him was a real cup and actually had a chip in it, while on the pale fawn carpet before his eyes was a rather dirty plimsoll.

Mr Cowgill got to his feet and picked up the shoe and then went over to the window and opened it as wide as possible and the roar of the early morning traffic came thudding into his ears.

'It can't be real. It *has* to be a dream,' said Mr Cowgill and pinched himself. 'It *IS* real,' he said, 'it is, it is . . . Sammy come back!'

But the striped wall-paper remained obstinately firm and solid.

On the other side of it Sammy was facing two gentlemen who were slowly rising to their feet. He had, he saw at that moment, completely misjudged the lay-out of the flats for instead of finding himself on the landing by the lift he was now in the kitchen of Mr Dimitriadi.

'Oh crumbs,' said Sammy, 'excuse me . . .'

He turned towards the wall, bracing himself to walk through it but even as he did so he knew it was too late for his own hand had become flesh and blood again and his feet, one of them minus a shoe, were as heavy as they had ever been.

'Crumbs,' agreed Mr Dimitriadi. 'Exactly, my young friend. Won't you sit down? I think you already know my friend and associate Mr Black . . .'

And he nodded towards the man at his side who smiled grimly as he said, 'So, we meet once more. Well Mr D., I think at last the luck runs in our favour. We have a hostage! You are our prisoner, Sammy Jenkins, and our prisoner you will remain until your friends give us the Unicorn. The last Unicorn? Yes?'

'Never,' said Sammy, which was extremely brave of him in the circumstances. 'Never, never, NEVER.'

'We shall see,' said Mr Black and he nodded to Mr Dimitriadi, who began to arrange his felt-tipped pens on the table before him while Sammy watched him, his heart thundering.

Mr Cowgill had no idea how long he sat holding the chipped coffee cup before he made up his mind. Then he got to his feet and with Sammy's shoe in one hand he walked out of the flat which had been his sanctuary and knocked on another front door.

'Sammy's gone,' he said to the person who answered him, 'vanished clean through the wall and I'm worried, Princess. You're the only person I can turn to for help. You *are* a Princess, aren't you?'

'In a manner of speaking,' said the small O Pear girl, 'so you are awake at last. Ah well, it had to happen. But now the real battle will begin and I had hoped so much that it could be avoided, as I do not like fighting.'

'I don't understand any of it,' said Mr Cowgill, 'but I will fight for you for ever. What must I do?'

'Go to the next door flat, Number 21, and ask Nell to join us. I will go for my Uncle, Mr Rhadaman. He has great powers and he will do all that he can, but this is White Magic against Black. Are you frightened?'

'Yes,' said Mr Cowgill honestly, 'because I don't understand what's going on. Is there truly a Unicorn, or did I dream it?'

'No, there is a Unicorn, the last Unicorn which looks for its Elysian Fields, that is, its sanctuary. Nell will tell you where it hides. Now go and go quickly.'

'I don't understand . . .' said Mr Cowgill, shaking his head. 'I don't understand anything that's happened, but I'll do what you say, because *you* say it. I'm not really mad am I?'

'No,' the O Pear girl said gently, 'not at all. Now go and go quickly for there is a great deal to be done if Sammy and the Unicorn are to be saved . . .'

And she gave him a gentle push towards the front door of Nell's grandmother's flat.

12. *Dangerous Magic*

To Sammy it seemed as if the world was going round and round in great dark circles. He was vaguely aware that Mr Dimitriadi had got down on his knees and was drawing some strange patterns on the kitchen floor with his felt-tipped pens while Mr Black, his arms folded across his chest, was standing back and smiling.

Mr Dimitriadi said breathlessly, 'You escaped from me once, but never again because now you're my prisoner, for always.'

'No, I'm not,' said Sammy, 'the Unicorn will rescue me, just you wait and see.'

'Which is exactly what I intend to do,' replied Mr D., 'only to be on the safe side we'd better imprison you in a place that is more strongly fortified than this place. Have you any suggestions Mr Black?'

'At the bottom of the River Thames, perhaps?' replied Mr Black with a chuckle. He spoke in such a pleasant tone of voice that for a second Sammy didn't realise just what these words implied and then he really did feel scared, more scared than he had ever been in his life before and he opened his mouth to shout for help and he tried to make a run for the door, but absolutely nothing happened. He heard a very faint squeak which was all his lungs could manage and his feet appeared to be glued to the bright red linoleum.

'Tut, tut,' said Mr Dimitriadi, waving one fat finger under Sammy's terrified nose. 'You're surrounded my boy, my magic symbols are all around you holding you firmly within my power. No, no, Mr Black, there is no need for us to dispose of the lad entirely, but your mentioning the Thames has given me an excellent idea. Crossing water always puts any pursuers off the scent so we'll make for a nice handy island, an uninhabited one naturally. I'll have a quick look through my road map in a moment. But first I must write a short note to the Bates girl so that she can pass it on to the Unicorn. Now let me see, where would be an appropriate place for it to surrender?'

Mr Dimitriadi tapped his little pointed teeth with

his felt tipped pen, his head enquiringly on one side, his small eyes glowing so that he looked for all the world like a plump, self-satisfied black cat.

'I'll get your stuff packed up,' said Mr Black, 'I take it you won't be staying on here?'

'No, rather not. Once we have the Unicorn safe and sound there'll be no point in hanging around. I'm sick and tired of London anyway, searching for that dratted creature day in and day out wasn't my idea of fun. It was all right for *you*, you quite enjoyed your job.'

In spite of everything Sammy couldn't help asking in a thin bat-like squeak, 'Is that why you came here to Leo Mansions?'

'Yes, indeed,' replied Mr Dimitriadi who was now in an excellent temper as he had at last captured (or *nearly* captured) the Unicorn. 'We had tried every possible lead up till that time; Unicorn Place, Unicorn Mews, the Unicorn General Stores, Unicorn Buildings, even a magazine called the Unicorn Press, and all to no avail. There was never so much as a sniff of the dratted thing. Unicorn House and Unicorn Gardens were our very last hope and in both of those places we came across just a hint, just the merest suggestion that we might be on the right track.'

'Both?' said Sammy's squeaky voice in astonishment.

'Hush do,' said Mr Dimitriadi who had begun to scribble rapidly. 'There, yes, very fine. It may not be a very brave creature, but it has got a great deal of vanity and I don't think it will be able to withstand my little note. Yes, both my dear boy. That surprises you, doesn't it? To be perfectly honest with you, I don't quite understand it myself, for why should there be a hint of the Unicorn at that extremely ugly modern building in the City of London? We neither of us know the answer to that question, but we had to seize on any clue, however faint it might be, and so Mr Black got a job there, a job he really liked as he's always been a man who enjoys proving his strength. In our circles he's often referred to as the Black Knight.'

Sammy shivered a little at these words and his eyes turned towards Mr Black who was coming into the room carrying a large suitcase as though it weighed nothing at all.

'Thank you, thank you,' murmured Mr Dimitriadi, 'my rent is all paid up and the gas and electricity are turned off so if we leave the key in the front door nobody will think it odd that I have vanished. Now where's my atlas? Ah yes . . .' and he flicked busily through the pages humming softly to himself.

'You'll never get away with this, never,' squeaked Sammy. 'Somebody will rescue me and then I shall tell them about everything.'

'Tell away, tell away,' said Mr Dimitriadi with a wide smile. 'Nobody will believe you, I can assure you of that. Oh what a stroke of luck it was to capture you. You could, of course, save everybody a great deal of trouble by telling us now where the Unicorn is hidden . . .'

He paused, one fat finger on the map and Mr Black, looming up behind him, fingered a sinister looking bulge in the side of his coat.

'N-n-o,' said Sammy.

He was sure inside himself that if only he could play for time something might yet be done to rescue both himself and the Unicorn. They had been in tight corners before and somehow managed to wriggle out of them, added to which there was the very faint chance that Mr Cowgill might do something to help.

Although it wasn't much of a hope, as that gentleman apparently still fondly believed that all that had happened was part of his imagination. However . . . and Sammy took a deep breath and looked fixedly at the wall while Mr Dimitriadi sighed and shrugged and said, 'You're a very stupid boy and extremely stubborn.'

'Let me . . .' said Mr Black, taking a half step forward with his hand raised.

'No. No violence here, it's too tricky. Later perhaps . . .'

Mr Dimitriadi shut the atlas, put it back neatly on the bookshelf and then took a key out of his pocket and signed to Mr Black, who took the note and the key and for a man of his size and weight, walked surprisingly quietly across the flat to the front door and opened it a crack. Sammy made a tremendous effort to shout, but only managed to produce a squeak and then Mr Black had slid the note through Mrs Bates' letter box and recrossed the landing, put the front door key in the key hole of Number 22 and rejoined Mr Dimitriadi, who had stepped inside the circle with Sammy.

'Splendid. *In* you get,' said Mr Dimitriadi, 'and *off* we go. I've chosen such a pretty little island, Sammy. I'm sure you'll enjoy your stay there . . .'

For a moment nothing happened and then the drawings on the red lino seemed to twist and leap and then to merge into a dancing, wreathing mist which whirled faster and faster until the three figures in their midst became indistinct too and then vanished completely and there was nothing at all to show that they had ever existed and the only sound was the roar of the traffic in the Earls Court Road.

It was at this precise second that first the telephone started ringing down in the basement flat and secondly that the little O Pear girl pushed Mr Cowgill out of his flat (at least the flat in which he had been staying) and towards the front door of No 21 and knocked on it loudly.

'Oh,' said Nell, looking extremely startled, 'I say, you do look ever so much better, but you shouldn't be here.'

'Well I am,' said Mr Cowgill, 'and it's urgent. Sammy's vanished.'

'Oh, not again,' said Nell, 'Oh,' she looked round distractedly, 'Well you'd better come in. Granny's having her bath so it's more or less safe,' and she pulled him into the front room.

It took a great deal of explaining on Mr Cowgill's part to make Nell grasp exactly what had occurred, as to begin with she couldn't get it out of her mind that Sammy must have become more and more invisible until there had been nothing left of him at all.

'So you know the O Pear girl,' Nell said when the muddle had finally been untangled, 'she's awfully nice isn't she?'

'*Awfully*,' agreed Mr Cowgill fervently. 'She's gone to get her uncle as she is certain he can help to get Sammy back.'

'Thank goodness for that,' said Nell. 'I've met him and he's a dear old man. He's got an antique shop in the Portobello Road and he and the O Pear girl took me down there yesterday. He's got dozens of little unicorn statues and I told him a bit about our Unicorn. Only a bit. Well, a bit more than a bit,' and Nell looked decidedly guilty. She had meant to own up to Sammy about giving away so much of their secret, but now there was no Sammy to unburden herself to and Nell felt a shiver of uneasiness run down her back.

There was a slithering sound and a pile of letters came through the letter box and Nell went to get them, rather glad of something to do as she knew she'd gone very pink. Most of the letters looked rather dull, although there was one addressed to her grandmother in her father's writing, so Nell put it on the top of the pile as it was obviously the most important and then she saw a note with her name on it and she tore it open. It was very short and to the point.

'Tell the Unicorn that we have Sammy as a hostage. We will exchange IT for the boy. If it does not agree —and we know that it's a coward—the boy will die. Our chosen meeting place is the top of the Shell Building at midnight.' And it was signed with a curious looking symbol.

Mr Cowgill took one look at Nell's face which had gone quite as white as the mantelpiece and snatched the paper out of her hand and read it. Outside on the landing there was a wheezing sound and then a clank, clank as the lift arrived and the doors were opened. Three people got out, the O Pear girl, a very elderly gentleman with a silky white beard and Sammy's Uncle Ted. All three of them made for the front door of Number 21.

'Y-y-y-yes,' said an ashen-faced Nell.

'Excuse me one moment Miss and you Sir,' said Uncle Ted, 'but could I have a word with this young lady urgently?'

'By all means,' said the elderly gentleman.

'It's about Sammy,' said Uncle Ted, 'I suddenly started getting very anxious about him just a few minutes ago and then I had a telephone call . . .' he swallowed and wiped his hand across his forehead,

'I'd appreciate it if you'd get him for me.'

Nell couldn't think of a single thing to either do or say. She had, as it were, a foot in the world of magic and a foot in the ordinary everyday world and now for the first time since the adventure had begun those two worlds had collided head on and poor Nell was too bewildered to even begin to try and sort them out . . . she could only stare with her mouth open and it was the elderly gentleman who came to her rescue by saying, 'Ah, your nephew Sammy Jenkins I suppose? I'm so sorry Mr Jenkins, but the boy has gone on an errand for me. I know I should have asked your permission first, but it was an urgent matter of business and Sammy is such a trustworthy boy, and, alas, there are so few of *them* about these days. He may be gone for some little while I fear . . .' and the elderly gentleman's gaze flickered towards Nell who was still standing with her mouth wide open. 'Allow me to present both my apologies and my card . . .'

'Yes, but, I say . . .' stuttered Uncle Ted and then he glanced at the card and his eyebrows went right up into his hair. 'Here, I know your name, sir. You're the Chairman of our Landlords.'

'I am indeed,' the elderly gentleman said with a slight bow, 'among many other things. And I can assure you Mr Jenkins that no harm will come to Sammy on his little mission and that he will be restored to you in perfectly good order later, er perhaps *quite* late, in the day. My business associates will take good care of him, *I* shall see to that.'

He spoke so firmly that Uncle Ted could only blink and nod his head.

'And how are the sash cords coming along?' asked the elderly gentleman.

'Very well,' said Uncle Ted, 'well then, if you'll excuse me . . .'

'Don't worry. And once more my apologies for my very high-handed action.'

'Not at all,' said Uncle Ted. 'Not at all, I'm sure,' and he went off to the lift shaking his head and marvelling at the way that the Chairman of the Landlords knew about the sash cords.

'The key is in the lock,' whispered the O Pear girl.

'Which means they've gone,' said the elderly gentleman, 'just as I feared. Well my boy you look a great deal better, at least that's something.'

'Sir,' gulped Mr Cowgill, who had just tiptoed out from the living room as he had heard the bath water running away and felt that it was high time he left No. 21. 'Sir,' what are *you* doing here?'

'Hm,' the elderly gentleman snorted, 'so this is where you've been hiding yourself my lad! A fine hue and cry there's been in the City about your vanishing act, why the place has been in turmoil. Old Boxikins has been going mad thinking you've been giving secrets away left, right and all the rest of it. Don't tell me that you're the fellow my great-niece has been rambling on about!'

'*Uncle*,' protested the O Pear girl going quite scarlet and at the same time Mr Cowgill's cheeks turned just as red and he shuffled his feet and looked everywhere but at the O Pear girl.

'Ho, ho, ho,' said the elderly gentleman and hastily blew his nose. '*I* see. Although it would have saved a great deal of time and trouble if I'd known that all along. However that's neither here nor there.'

'No it isn't,' burst out Nell, who had been listening to all this with her head going from side to side as she stared at first one person and then another, 'no it isn't. They've got Sammy. Please, please *do* something. They're going to kill him.'

'Never,' said the elderly gentleman firmly, 'they won't go to those lengths. Well, first things first, where's that Unicorn of yours, eh? Still got it safe and sound, silly creature that it is?'

'In the best coal house,' said Nell, 'but I had this letter and they *are* going to kill Sammy, look!' and she thrust the note into his hand just as Mrs Bates called out, 'El-ea-nor who are you talking to, dear?'

The elderly gentleman seized Mr Cowgill by the sleeve and drew him out onto the landing and turned the key to open the front door of Mr Dimitriadi's flat, saying over his shoulder as he did so, 'Tell your grandmother that you will be spending the day with us, although with her permission naturally, and that you may be returning rather late . . .'

'But,' said Nell.

'My child,' the elderly gentleman shook his white head and smiled, 'I am Mr Rhadaman and I am the one who is responsible for the Unicorn and its Elysian Fields, its sanctuary. You can trust me, I promise. We must save Sammy and, if possible, the Unicorn as well. It is, after all, the *last* Unicorn . . .'

Nell looked at him and then at the O Pear girl and lastly at Mr Cowgill. She had to trust somebody it was true, but all the same it was a very big decision to make.

'O.K.,' said Nell, and turned back to meet her grandmother, who was just emerging from the bathroom in her pink dressing-gown with a large plastic flowered cap over her curlers.

13. *Into Battle*

'Well,' said the Unicorn, cavorting round and round on its sharp little hooves, '*I* don't know. I'm not sure I'm up to it and that's a fact. My magic's gone off a lot lately. I'm not the creature I was and that's the truth.'

It was indeed, for there were flecks of grey in its coat and even its long pointed horn was no longer as white and shining as it had once been.

'The children saved *you*,' replied Mr Rhadaman, 'you owe *them* a favour now.'

There was a rather embarrassing silence during which the Unicorn looked at its reflection in the speckled mirror and everybody else looked at their feet. It had been an extremely tiring day during which the O Pear girl had gone out to buy sandwiches, pork pies, oranges and bottles of fizzy lemon and there had been long, somewhat fruitless discussions on how to find and rescue Sammy.

'You *must* do it,' Mr Rhadaman said firmly, 'I have done everything I can to protect *you* after all. I worked my way up at Unicorn House from being a clerk to getting on the Board of Directors so that I could be on hand should you come there. I started up an Antique shop in the Portobello Road specialising in Unicornia . . .'

'Uni what?' Nell asked with interest. She was dreadfully anxious about Sammy, but with her three new allies she was not as frightened as she had been.

'Unicornia,' the Unicorn replied, 'that means anything to do with *me*, you know. How very interesting that must be,' and it perked up a little.

'It's a very limited field actually,' said Mr Rhadaman, 'and it brought no results from you at all! Not so much as a sniff. *And* I became Chairman of the Landlords here at Leo Mansions should you . . .'

'All right, all right,' the Unicorn said sulkily, 'but you've no idea how difficult it's been for me! And I'm getting sick and tired of all this running away. Once upon a time I was admired and respected and looked up to. But what am I now? A refugee! And even if we *do* rescue Sammy from Them what kind of future shall I have? There'll always be somebody after me, hunting me down.'

'Sanctuary,' mused Mr Rhadaman, 'ah, it becomes increasingly difficult for all of us to find *that* in this modern world. Even budgerigars, goldfish and turtles have to run for their lives . . .' and he shot a look at Nell who went very pink, and then went on, 'but you and I are old, Unicorn, older than time itself. Perhaps we should move on and make way for what is to come after us.'

'Ha!' The Unicorn's great white eyes turned to look across the somewhat crowded coal house. 'But what *will* come after us? Rockets and space travel. Instant meals in plastic bags—which nobody can get rid of—taller blocks of flats with larger colour television sets in them. Bigger, noisier, dirtier cars. Quite soon there'll be no room for magic at all. Ha!' And it snorted furiously.

'As long as there are young people there will always be space enough and time enough for magic,' Mr Rhadaman replied gently, 'the world may change, but children don't. And you don't want to vanish for ever on a sour note do you? Do you want to be remembered as a coward, as a craven runaway from the field of battle? *You*!'

The Unicorn shook back its greying mane, tossed its head and swished its long tail while the O Pear girl and Mr Cowgill held hands and Nell held her breath.

'O very *well*,' it said suddenly. 'If you put it like that—give me Sammy's shoe, Sir Cowgill.'

Mr Cowgill got up and took over the rather battered plimsoll and the Unicorn sniffed it, rolled its eyes and stiffened.

'Yes,' it said softly, 'yes—wait—wait . . .'

Everybody did as they were told and there was not

a sound in the coal house until the Unicorn went on so softly that it was like a sigh.

'He is not so very far away I think and there is a trail . . . yes, yes . . .'

'I'm going with you,' said Nell, scrambling to her feet.

'No,' Mr Rhadaman caught hold of her arm, 'this will not be a sight for children or girls. What is needed now is a Knight, a White Knight,' and he picked up the pikestaff which Sammy had absent-mindedly brought back from the Tower of London and looked at Mr Cowgill.

'Very well,' said Mr Cowgill, 'I will be your White Knight. It's always been my dream to gain my spurs in a Battle and to win the hand of a Princess. It's exactly like the stories I used to read when I was a boy.'

'But this isn't a story,' Mr Rhadaman said. 'This is *real.* There will be great forces massed against you for you will be fighting dangerous magic. White does not *always* win against Black. This is not a Battle to undertake lightly.'

Mr Cowgill looked from face to face and then stiffened his shoulders.

'Nevertheless I shall fight. The Unicorn will guide me.'

And he climbed onto the chilly back of the shivering, shaking Unicorn who for one pin, let alone two, would have vanished if it could, and couched the pikestaff under his arm as naturally as if he had been trained to use a lance all his life, for somehow it seemed to fit instantly in his grasp.

'No,' cried the O Pear girl, 'oh my gracious-uncle-in-white-magic you can't let him go like this. He may never return.'

'Please, please let us go too,' implored Nell.

'How about it?' asked the Unicorn, shivering more than ever.

'No,' Mr Rhadaman said sternly, 'we must obey the rules of the game. This will be a Battle between Black and White, one knight against the other. But we shall fight too in our way. Child, niece, give me your hands and hold on tightly.'

They did as they were ordered and at the same moment the Unicorn and its rider spun and spun in a white cloud and the walls of the best coal house seemed to disolve into mist as Mr Rhadaman cried out in an echoing voice, 'All white creatures of the air obey me. Aid me. Come to my side and fight for us against our Enemy of the Night.'

And at his cry a shiver ran through the roof tops of London. A warm wind sprang up from the South and a chill, bitter wind from the North and the winds rushed towards each other sweeping up their allies as they went. It was as though a secret message was being passed from place to place, a message for which each creature had been on the alert during the last twenty-four hours.

'To me, to me,' called the South Wind.

'To me, to me,' growled the North Wind.

Heads turned, ears pricked, fur grew stiff and feathers ruffled up and down the streets, avenues, squares and crescents of London. Cats arched their backs and spat, dogs growled and complained deep in their throats and even the grey rats and white mice stopped what they were doing and listened. Cart horses stamped their great shaggy hooves, ponies rolled their eyes and the sleek thoroughbreds in the Royal stables shook their heads impatiently. The pigeons in Trafalgar Square took to their wings and whirled upwards in great flapping clouds and the starlings stopped chattering.

Tortoises, hedgehogs, guinea-pigs and field mice stood motionless and the ducks and drakes on St James' Park abandoned their nests and clucked and called to each other and even the fish beneath them formed into shoals and swam backwards and forwards listening. A porpoise, flipping its careless way up through the oily waters of the Pool of London, paused and then dived deep into the mud and the thousands and thousands of sparrows stopped quarrelling and turned their heads.

And so a second great unease settled on the wild life, and the not so wild life, of Greater London as each creature listened to the shrill, distant signals that they alone could hear and even the carrion crows folded their ragged wings and were still. No human ears picked up the thin fluting call as it was too high for them and if some of the homeward bound commuters were aware of anything strange and unusual in the air above their heads they put it all down to the Equinox, which is always an unsettled time of the year.

But still the signals went on. To some creatures it now said, 'A battle is about to commence and your help is needed urgently.' And to others it said, 'This is not *your* fight, but you may stay and watch if you wish to.'

The call criss-crossed the Thames a dozen times and reached a small island where it sang through the dark bushes and round the heads of Mr Dimitriadi and Mr Black who were counting off the minutes to midnight. They looked at each other and Mr Dimitriadi said furiously, 'It's Rhadaman and he means to make a fight of it. All right, let him and then we'll see who's master here once and for all!'

Sammy, imprisoned and helpless inside his black magic ring could only watch as the small stout man began to draw symbols on the ground, but as he did so there was a sudden fluttering of wings behind him and two white swans took to the air and flew off into the night sky. Mr Dimitriadi turned to look at them and then said even more furiously, 'Oh well, if *that's* the way they want it . . .'

He held up his arms, his fingers outstretched and stiff as he muttered under his breath and at once all over London creatures of stone stirred into life. They moved their shoulders, spread their wings and unsheathed their claws as their long, sharp ears pricked up. One by one, as stealthily as cats, the gargoyles slid away from their roof tops, their black eyes shining. They slithered down the sides of churches and cathedrals. They clambered off roofs and away from drain-pipes with their long necks and cruel beaks outstretched. For five hundred, a thousand years and even more they had been imprisoned, but now at last they were free again. They gathered in half-dozens and then dozens and then by the score, squealing and yowling and yelping in their high shrill voices. All the hideous Black Magic creatures that had been incarcerated in stone over the centuries answered to the battle cry which had at long last sounded in their ears and brought them back to life. They soared up into the dark racing night sky, wheeling and gathering strength until they were like a great black cloud blotting out the moon.

'They are strong,' whispered Mr Rhadaman, 'they are a great force on the side of Dangerous Magic. Come to me, come to me oh my Creatures of Light and fight our Enemy of Darkness . . .'

And his cry too was answered as in a hundred lofts

pigeons and turtle doves stirred and murmured softly to each other, while out on the lakes, ponds and marshes the swans lifted up their sleek white heads and then spread their great wings.

'White against Black,' said Mr Rhadaman, 'good magic against bad. So it has always been. Sometimes one will win and at other times another.'

'Who will win *now*?' asked Nell, clutching on tightly to Mr Rhadaman's arm. They seemed to be on the top of a very tall building indeed, even taller than Unicorn House and the whole of London appeared to be stretched out below them. They were, in fact, on the roof of the Shell Building, which stands on the south bank of the Thames and from which the view is truly magnificent, but neither Nell nor the O Pear girl were in the mood to appreciate this.

'We must wait and find out,' Mr Rhadaman replied gravely. 'Look, look—over there . . .'

One lone figure appeared against the darkness. It was Mr Cowgill astride the no-longer shivering Unicorn, for now that it had the scent of battle in its nostrils the creature had lost its fear. They soared over the rooftops, the pikestaff couched under Mr Cowgill's steady arm. Beneath him he could see the last of the home-going traffic and the lights of the Embankment shifting backwards and forwards in the wind. He tightened his grip and whispered against the streaming mane of the Unicorn.

'WE shall win. We MUST win. To me, to me . . .' and his voice rose to a shout.

And at the same moment Mr Black reared up from his small dark island. He was wearing a full suit of armour, provided by Mr Dimitriadi, and was riding a coal black horse which had until a few seconds ago been standing sedately in Trafalgar Square with King Charles the First on its back. The statue of the King, its dignity not in the least impaired by this high-handed action, was left in mid-air, but nobody noticed this as the drivers swirling round its plinth were far too busy about their own affairs. So the black horse kicked and fretted and then flung up its head as sharp spurs were driven into its flanks.

The dark racing clouds streamed behind the Houses of Parliament as the Black Knight came riding across the sky from the south while the White Knight raced towards the river from the North, his trousers and his tie flapping.

'Armour,' cried Mr Rhadaman, 'this must be a fair fight . . .'

Mr Cowgill—and the Unicorn which was in a tremendous state of excitement by this time—sagged slightly as Mr Cowgill's neat City suit was suddenly encased in shining white steel. Neither of them noticed that above their heads a great black storm was gathering as the gargoyles swept down, rank after rank with their necks and beaks and claws outstretched for the kill.

'To me, to me,' shouted the Black Knight, 'all creatures of the Great Darkness to me!'

'To me, to me,' cried Mr Cowgill throwing back his head, his heart hammering, 'all creatures of the Light, aid me!' And even as he spoke he wondered how he knew the right words.

'Up boys and at 'em,' whispered the Unicorn, 'oh how it brings it all back to me. The creak of the harness, the weight of the armour, the cry of the battlefield. Ah, happy days when chivalry . . .'

'There isn't going to be any chivalry if you don't shut up,' said Mr Cowgill breathlessly.

'Sorry,' said the Unicorn and for once in its long life did as it was ordered without argument.

Mr Cowgill steadied his pikestaff and the Unicorn with a great shuddering snort streaked across the surging, white tipped waters of the Thames.

'Mine is the Victory,' roared the Black Knight and levelling his lance rushed downwards.

The Unicorn tried to swerve, but it was a split second too late and Mr Cowgill felt a hot stinging blow on his shoulder. He clutched at the icy cold white mane and groaned and the Unicorn said huskily, 'Hold on, hold on. Here comes something I learnt in my last fight . . .' And it ducked and swirled sideways and to the horrified watchers on the top of the Shell Building appeared to go clean under the Black Knight's snorting charger.

'Well done, oh well done,' said Mr Rhadaman, who in the excitement of the battle had completely forgotten that Nell and the O Pear girl were not supposed to be witnessing all this. 'Did you see that move? That was the Premier Feint. Only the very *best* Unicorns were ever taught to do it. Oh well *done*!'

'Well done indeed,' the O Pear girl agreed shakily.

'Yes, but look,' cried Nell and pointed upwards.

The hovering cloud of gargoyles had waited long enough to have their revenge and their thin yelping cries rose to a shriek as they saw the White Knight slip away from his death. Down they swooped, claws, talons, beaks outstretched, their black eyes glittering as they went into the attack.

The Unicorn swerved and dipped and Mr Cowgill aimed his lance over and over again at the tormenting, whining, shrieking, yowling host which pecked now at him, now at the heaving flanks of the Unicorn.

But still their long pointed teeth sank into his armour and into the Unicorn's flying mane and tail and they even singed its delicate hooves so that it skittered sideways across the night sky, losing height as it did so until the flying spray from the river flecked its labouring sides.

'The Unicorn grows weaker,' whispered Mr Rhadaman.

'We are winning,' shouted Mr Dimitriadi gleefully and in his joy he stepped out of the Black Magic Circle and broke it. At once Sammy felt all his energy flowing back and he took a very deep breath and then yelled at the top of his voice.

'Help, help. It's me, Sammy Jenkins. HELP.'

There was a fluttering sound in the rushes and then another noise which sounded like sheets being ripped apart and above his head white wings flapped, circled and then rose up into the night sky, growing smaller and smaller until they looked like snow flakes. The two great swans flew on, calm and apparently serene as they were joined by more and more of their number and also welcomed into their ranks white pigeons and turtle doves. And further down the Thames on the battlements of the Tower of London, the three ebony black ravens, danced from claw to claw in their fury at not being able to join in the fight.

'I'd show 'em, I'd show 'em,' cawed the eldest, all its feathers ruffled and stiff. 'A left feint then a right wheel and attack from below. That's the way to do it.'

'Go it Unicorn,' cawed the second bird. 'Oh why do they have to clip our wings! I'd like to clip their feet and see how *they* like it.'

'I thought you weren't all that keen on the Unicorn,' put in the third and youngest raven, 'when it came on that surprise visit it called us Civil Servants if you remember.'

'It also called us black in feather, but white of heart. Don't you realise this is a great battle, you—you—you undersized crow? Now come on, all together. One, two, three. *Go it Unicorn!*'

The great flock of white birds wheeled up and up so that a graceful white fan seemed to be first shaken open and then flicked shut and transformed into a shining spear, each bird in its allotted place. For a moment the spear, shivering slightly, paused and then wooooosh and it was arrowing downwards.

'They're coming,' shouted Mr Rhadaman, 'hold up Unicorn, hold up . . .'

Both the Unicorn and Mr Cowgill were really past knowing what was happening above their heads, for by this time they had at least fifty gargoyles clinging to them with claws and teeth, dragging them down into the dark, choppy waters, while the Black Knight, grinning behind his vizor, couched his lance and moved in for the kill.

But Mr Dimitriadi saw and he covered his glowing green eyes with his podgy hands and fell flat on his face.

'Hurry, hurry,' yelled Sammy, who like the ravens was dancing from foot to foot. 'Oh *quick!*'

The frothing waves touched the Unicorn's skittering hooves and dragged at its long tail and washed over the yelping gargoyles, making them look blacker still.

'Once more, once more,' Mr Cowgill muttered, his lungs heaving and he wrenched the Unicorn sideways as a bigger wave reared up towards them. It was not at all a graceful movement, but somehow wallowing and snorting the Unicorn did as it was ordered and so gained a second's respite and in that second the white thunderbolt descended. Each and every bird picked out its own particular black enemy and attacked it. The weight of the gargoyles fell away and Mr Cowgill, more by luck than any kind of judgment, pointed his pikestaff upwards and shoved with his last remaining strength. He hit something very solid, so solid that the pikestaff snapped in two and dimly he heard, above all the other noise of battle, a terrible cry.

'Ahhhhhh,' shrieked the Black Knight caught off balance.

His horse reared under him and before he could stop himself the Black Knight slid backwards and then with a tremendous crash fell on top of the squirming, squealing gargoyles and with the enormous weight of his armour drove them with a great uprush of spray deep into the Thames. The gargoyles, never the bravest of creatures, immediately abandoned the fight as they lunged and pushed and bit at each other in the black mud of the river bed and then, each battling for its own survival, rose up again in a tangled wreathing mass carrying willy-nilly the Black Knight with them. He was born aloft into the scurrying clouds, carried over the Houses of Parliament and abandoned without ceremony on the top of Unicorn House where he froze instantly into stone and where he remains to this day, his mouth wide open under his vizor. Perhaps some time far into the future he may come to life again, but meantime there he remains and a very fitting gargoyle he makes. As for his horse, it was so relieved to be released that it galloped back across the sky to its rightful place and settled down peacefully under King Charles the First as though it had never been away.

And while all this was going on Mr Cowgill managed to say in a very faint voice. 'Up, up, oh Unicorn I'm nearly spent . . .'

'Not half as spent as I am,' replied the Unicorn, its sides heaving. 'I'm far too old for this kind of thing, but all the sâme I think we've won. Yes, what is it . . .?'

And it bent a very battered ear towards a swan that was streaming past like a yacht in full sail.

The swan hooted softly, pecked at a piggy little gargoyle which shot off into the darkness, and then serenely flapped on its way.

'Oh, is *that* all,' said the Unicorn, 'well I knew that already, thank you *very* much . . . hold on Sir Cowgill. We go to rescue Sammy,' and it set off after the swan, groaning quite horribly.

Actually it limped rather than flew and landed extremely heavily on the small island where Sammy had been kept prisoner. Mr Cowgill holding his shoulder, rolled off its back and fell to his knees. Before him he saw a small, tubby man lying flat on his face and a very white-faced boy.

''lo,' said the Unicorn huskily.

'Hallo,' replied Sammy, equally breathless, 'you took your time getting here.'

'Did the best I could,' said the Unicorn, shaking the cold sweat out of its eyes. 'And anyway you've no idea of what we've been through, Sir Cowgill and me. We've been engaged in a great battle. A battle in which we were nearly defeated and in which we suffered very badly. Look at the state I'm in. We're in. It's all very well for you to loll about watching—by the way where *is* here?'

'Battersea Park,' said Sammy, hitting Mr Cowgill on the back and shaking his very trembly mailed fist at the same time. 'On the island in the middle of the lake. How did you manage to find me?'

'Followed the swan. Apparently it nests hereabouts and you and Nell fed it quite recently and spoke politely to it. Swans appreciate that kind of thing, like us Unicorns do. Of course I knew you were perfectly *safe*, I could sense that in my bones—oh they do ache—and I'd've found you anyway in a very short while as I was close on your trail, still it was nice to be able to take a short cut.'

'Thank you,' said Sammy somewhat indistinctly as he had buried his face in the creature's wringing wet mane, 'thank you for rescuing me, I was jolly frightened, you know. It was ever so brave of you to fight like that.'

'It was nothing,' the Unicorn replied, sniffing furiously, 'I mean it was the least I could do. What is *that* over there?'

'Mr Dimitriadi, he's your Arch Enemy. Watch out for him, he's very dangerous.'

'Pooh, he's nothing to be scared of,' the Unicorn said quite jauntily, although like Mr Cowgill and Sammy he was still trembling violently. 'Hallo, there go my loyal troops,' and it lifted its battered white head as flight after flight of birds streamed overhead. 'Not a bad lot really, amateurs of course, but then you can't expect too much these days. Here, Sammy, watch out for my White Knight he looks a bit poorly . . .'

'You don't look too good yourself,' said Sammy in a somewhat high voice as he grabbed at Mr Cowgill, who had slumped forwards.

'*Nonsense*,' replied the Unicorn in an even more unsteady voice. 'I'm *perfectly* well. Nothing the matter with me. I've just won a great battle haven't

I? The greatest battle of my entire career. Why when I recall that Premier Feint which I executed to perfection I can only . . . oooooh.'

The Unicorn stopped speaking, gave a strange little sigh, rolled its beautiful eyes and without another sound crumpled at the knees and fainted dead away.

14. *The Elysian Fields*

There were, of course, a great many matters which still had to be attended to, but as there's nothing like a great battle—even if you happen to have won it—to tire you out, nobody felt like dealing with anything once the fight was over. Mr Rhadaman made a few hasty arrangements during which a white circle was firmly drawn round the quaking Mr Dimitriadi to keep him safe and Mr Cowgill, who like the Unicorn had fainted clean away, was removed of his armour and transported back to Leo Mansions with the O Pear to look after him.

'And what about us and it?' asked Sammy, his face quite stiff with exhaustion as he patted the apparently lifeless Unicorn.

'Bed,' said Mr Rhadaman firmly. 'We will meet tomorrow in a place of sanctuary. Where would be convenient for you?'

'The coal house,' said Sammy and yawned so widely that he heard his jaw crack. 'I say, it was a *smashing* fight wasn't it?'

'Smashing,' agreed Mr Rhadaman, 'are you ready? One, two, THREE . . .'

In spite of a very good night's sleep everybody was still very pale on the following morning, except for the Unicorn which looked positively grey, while Mr Cowgill had his arm in a sling. Mr Rhadaman was the last to arrive and his old eyes twinkled as he sat down on a cardboard box and surveyed the company.

'Well,' he said, 'let's get down to business. Dear me, it's just like a Board Meeting at Unicorn House, now what's first on the agenda?'

'Mr Dimitriadi,' said Nell, 'supposing he starts hunting the Unicorn again?'

'There's no need to worry about him. He's lost all his powers and can't scare anybody any more. However, I suppose he had better go somewhere. He can't stay on that little island for ever after all. So let me see . . . ah yes, I know the very place! Somewhere nice and safe where he can't do any more damage.'

And Mr Rhadaman got down on his knees a bit stiffly and wiped out the last of the chalk marks on the floor and drew a neat little pattern with a white felt-tipped pen. And as he did so a rotund, small figure who had, in fact, been waiting and expecting to be completely eliminated, found itself being whirled round and round and then carried quite painlessly from the island in the middle of Battersea Park to a much drier location. Luckily nobody happened to be walking their dogs in the Gardens when there was a sudden whirlpool of activity inside the small wicket fence and a new, gleaming white statue appeared. It was not as elegant as the Unicorn had been, it was indeed rather an abstract type of figure, although later on a great many people—some of them extremely artistic—said that it reminded them of a large white cat. Mr Dimitriadi-that-was had found a new home.

'I daresay he'll be perfectly happy there,' said Mr Rhadaman, 'plenty of fresh air, people to admire him, and no worries at all really.'

'But supposing there's another storm?' asked Nell, who still didn't feel too safe about this new arrangement.

'Lightning,' said Mr Rhadaman, 'very, very rarely strikes twice in the same place. And if it does it won't be for another thousand years at least and that's hardly likely to bother *us*. Next question?'

'Me,' said the Unicorn huskily. 'All right then, that's the problem of my Arch Enemy solved, but what about *me*?' I'm tired of all this hurly-burly and although I don't care to admit it, I *am* quite definitely growing older. That raven in the Tower told me I wasn't looking as young as I was once upon a time. It's a rude, uneducated bird, but there may be some truth in what it said. Well?'

'Ah,' Mr Rhadaman stroked his beard and smiled slightly, 'you've become almost mortal my friend, that's your trouble. Will you settle for a more restful middle age?'

'I might,' the Unicorn replied cautiously. 'I certainly don't appear to have much of a position in this modern, noisy world. Even that vulgar lion in the Zoo told me as much and my magic has nearly vanished. Nobody appreciates me any more,' and it sighed dolefully.

'We do,' said Nell.

'That's right,' agreed Sammy, a bit embarrassed.

'Too kind,' the Unicorn murmured.

'Then your solution is simple my friend,' said Mr Rhadaman, 'I shall remove your horn and you will be transformed into a pony. A very remarkable, unusual and beautiful pony, naturally. You will need someone like Nell to care for you and groom you, of course.'

'I'd rather it was her than anybody else. She's not bad at it,' the Unicorn said, with a sideways look at Nell who replied instantly, 'Oh Unicorn, do say yes. You know I love you and I've always wanted my very *own* pony. I'd look after you, really I would, for ever and ever.'

'It's not an easy decision,' the Unicorn said slowly as it studied itself in the mirror, 'I am, after all, the *last* Unicorn and it means giving up my horn . . .'

'Yes, but don't you see,' said Nell, stroking its grey edged mane and somewhat tattered coat, 'if you become a pony in the New Forest you'll be *safe*! It'll be just like your Elysium place because there are glades and trees there. And pools where you can see yourself and lots and lots of people to admire you too and none of them will want to hunt you, they'll only want to take your photograph and feed you. And I'll brush your coat until it's pure white again.

Oh say yes, Unicorn, say yes!'

The Unicorn hesitated a moment longer and as it looked at its straight white horn a single tear squeezed out of one sad white eye and then it sniffed and tossed back its mane and said.

'Oh very well, if you insist and if it will make everybody else happy who am I to say no? But what of the others?'

'There are no problems there,' said Mr Rhadaman. 'Sir Cowgill has proved himself in battle and won his Princess and together they will travel to their sunlit isles of Greece. I shall also retire and as for Sammy . . .'

'Yes,' said Sammy, jerking to attention for he was three parts asleep again.

'Your Elysian Fields have already started to materialise,' said Mr Rhadaman, his smile growing broader, 'as your father, who works I understand for a subsidiary company of the Unicorn Overseas Development Trust, has been recalled to this country. There has been quite a shake up since er . . .' he coughed delicately and then Sammy who had been staring at him quite goggle-eyed, leapt to his feet, all thoughts of sleep forgotten as he shouted, 'Go on, go on, what do you mean?'

'Well since industrial spying was suspected at Unicorn House, white magic, which works in very odd ways you know, has been very much on your side and with a bit of pulling here and there has brought your father back to work in this country. *And* promoted him. Your Uncle Ted had a phone call only last night from Kuwait, but the line was so bad he couldn't understand half of it. However quite soon now, any minute in fact, there should be another call to say that your father has landed at London Airport . . .'

'He never,' said Sammy, 'Has he? Has he *really* . . .?'

'I shouldn't be at all surprised,' said Mr Rhadaman gravely.

'Oh crumbs, oh crikey, oh gosh,' said Sammy, 'did you all hear that. I say!'

'Sammy I AM glad,' said Nell, 'isn't it smashing? It's all come out right in the end hasn't it? We've neither of us got mumps and the Unicorn's going to be my own special pony and Mr Cowgill's going to marry his Princess. Granny had a letter from Daddy yesterday saying I'd better come home this weekend because of being out of quarantine, but I didn't like to tell you until now. Oh Sammy I *am* glad.'

There was a great deal of hand-shaking and congratulation all round and even the Unicorn stopped gazing mournfully at its reflection and said huskily, 'Well that's all right then. I mean I couldn't leave until I knew you were all right. I always put duty first as you may have realised . . .'

'Mmm,' said Sammy, frowning quite horribly because otherwise he might have had to sniff or blow his nose, only he seemed to have lost his handkerchief. The Unicorn was vain and tiresome (and sometimes cowardly) but for some reason it was also very difficult to say goodbye to for ever.

'Well,' it said, snorting and throwing back its grey flecked mane, 'it's been very nice knowing all of you and I realise you've done your best for me, even if you are untrained in chivalry and knighthood. But it's time to move on. Me to my Elysian Fields and you to yours. I thank you for your aid good friends.'

It crossed its front legs and bowed its head and in spite of the peck marks in its coat and its torn mane and slightly mangled tail it had somehow never looked more beautiful, or more regal.

It was also, quite obviously, telling everybody—except Mr Rhadaman—that it was time to leave. Mr Cowgill and the O Pear girl and then Sammy and Nell lined up to say goodbye and once the coal house door had closed behind them the Unicorn wilted a bit and then snorted and swished its tail.

'I *hate* farewells,' it said. 'Well, so ends my last adventure and so ends the last unicorn. It's a pretty melancholy business you must admit!'

'Don't you believe it,' said Mr Rhadaman, 'your sort never die out. I may take your horn away now, but one day . . .'

'Yes?' said the Unicorn, 'oh that reminds me, and I hope I'm not a creature to forget its obligations, what about those birds, turtles and fish of the Caretaker Jenkins? I had some quite interesting chats with them and they tell me that officially they're not allowed in this place. Can nothing be done for them?'

'Certainly. As the Chairman of the Landlords I shall make it my place to rescind the notice about people not keeping pets here. But as I was saying . . .'

'Mmmm?' said the Unicorn in much the same tone as Sammy had used as it gazed at its reflection in the speckled mirror, 'Mmmm?'

'Nothing much,' replied Mr Rhadaman raising his hand to begin the spell which would remove the shining horn of the Unicorn, 'nothing much *really*. Only I feel deep down in my bones that somehow, somewhere that horn may well start to grow again. Even in this present world of ours we seem to need Unicorns. Are you ready?'

And at the same moment Sammy and Nell, who were supposed to be feeding the turtles but weren't, looked at each other and whispered.

'Goodbye Unicorn, see you again one day . . .'

While six storeys up Mr Cowgill and the O Pear girl, standing hand in hand, were saying softly, 'Good luck Unicorn. If it hadn't been for you *we* should never have met each other . . .'

'Hold still,' said Mr Rhadaman in the coal house.

'I'm doing my best,' said the Unicorn, fidgeting and shifting on its delicate hooves, 'you know in spite of everything I really feel quite sad to leave. After all I am the *last* Unicorn. One day though I may decide to come back, because I shouldn't be surprised if somebody may want me to fight a battle somewhere. I am *rather* special in my way.'

'You are indeed,' agreed Mr Rhadaman, 'and I wouldn't be surprised either. Now then brace yourself, Unicorn, because this is it. One, two, THREE . . .'